Los Angeles Review of Books

Quarterly Journal

Inaugural Issue, Fall 2013

The Los Angeles Review of Books is supported by PEN Center USA. The LARB Quarterly Journal is published quarterly by the Los Angeles Review of Books, 1614 S. Central Ave., Glendale, CA 91204. Printed in Los Angeles by Janet Klein / Sinclair Printing. Submissions for the Journal can be emailed to editorial@lareviewofbooks.org. Visit our website at www.lareviewofbooks.org. The LARB Quarterly Journal is a premium of the LARB Membership Program. Annual subscriptions are available. Go to www.lareviewofbooks/membership or email membership@lareviewofbooks.org for more information. Distribution through Publishers Group West. If you are a retailer and would like to order the LARB Quarterly Journal, call 800-788-3123 or email orderentry@perseusbooks.com. To place an ad in the LARB Quarterly Journal, email adsales@lareviewofbooks.org.

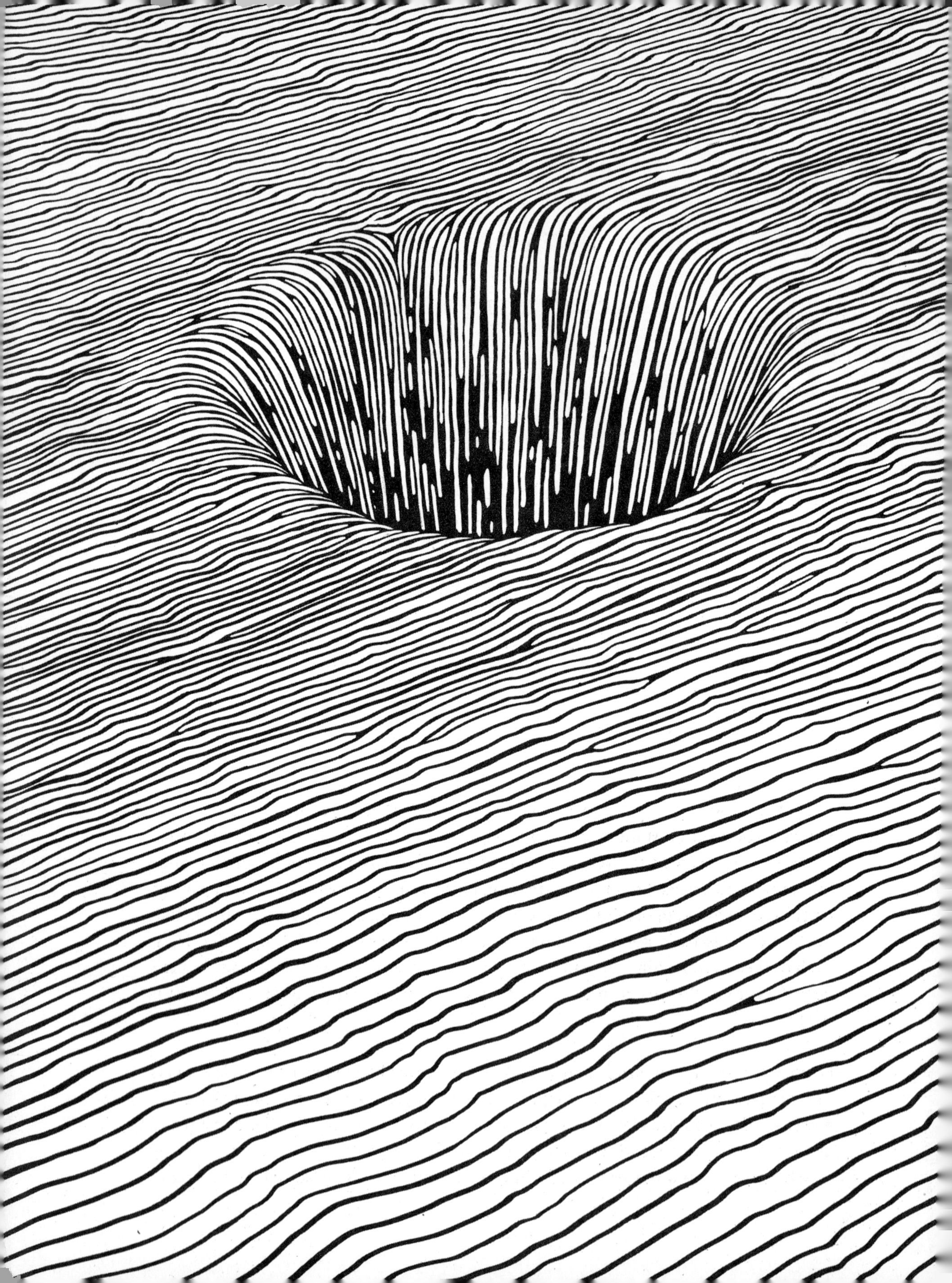

Papyralysis

JACOB MIKANOWSKI

"A book, gentlemen, is a stack of papers, held together by glue."

Colonel Friedrich Kraus
Good Soldier Svejk

"Papyr was whitish, flaccid, a derivative of cellulose, rolled out on cylinders and cut into rectangular sheets [...] No one knows exactly when and where the papyralysis epidemic broke out [...] In place of those great treasuries, those reservoirs of society's memory, lay mounds of gray, powdery ash."

Stanisław Lem
Memoirs Found in a Bathtub

We're living in a weird moment. Everything has become archivable. Our devices produce a constant record of our actions, our movements, our thoughts. Forget memory: if we wanted to, we could reconstruct every aspect of a life with an iPhone and some hard drives. But at the same time, physical archives seem to be fading away. Once, they were supported by a whole ecology of objects and institutions, including prints, presses, notebooks, letters, diaries, manuscripts, and marginalia. Now, each of these is vanishing, one after another. Letters don't get written. Handwriting's been forgotten. Presses crumble. Paper molders. And everyone agrees: the book is next to go.

Of course it won't happen all at once. Maybe it isn't even happening now. Digital books are increasingly popular — but paper books are more popular still. Publishing is a mess — unless you're a giant multinational or a thriving independent. Readership is in decline — but that depends on what you think ought to be read. Paper is a frustrating anachronism — and our offices and homes are full of it. The clash of technologies

BRENDAN MONROE

that we're living through is probably less a case of the silents vs. the talkies than of radio vs. TV. However popular e-readers become, paper books will still be able to carve out a space in their shadow, at least in the short term.

But how long will the short term last? It used to be possible to imagine books disappearing in the distant future. Now it feels like even money that it's going to happen within our lifetimes. I grew up doing everything with pencil and paper. Now I'd rather whittle a fence than write an essay longhand. Paper is starting to feel like a Luddite affectation, on par with mustache wax or making your own yogurt. Pretty soon, with no context to sustain it, it's going to slide into the realm of pure anachronism, the sort of thing you do to one-up your neighbors, and have to explain to your kids.

"Every part of the book has a history of its own."

Can we think our way back to a time before the great digitization? Before the Cloud? Before Google Glass and cortical implants and neuro-adaptive braille, before human uploads and the Hive? Before reading on, go get a book and hold it in front of you... Now, leaf through it. Notice the typeface. The symmetry. The geography of the ink. But be careful: it is liable to tear, or fall apart altogether.

This was the main way information was recorded and transmitted. What an amazing technology. Invented before gunpowder or the stirrup, the book lasted longer than the steam engine and the rotary phone. Every part of it was adapted for human use over hundreds of years of trial and error. Notice the height and the width of the spine, perfectly suited to the palm. Do you see the width of these pages? They're set in relation to our natural vision span, which relates in turn to the size of the macula in the human eye.

The materials that went into making a book could be selected to fulfill specific needs. They could be cheap and light or heavy and durable. A book made from vellum could easily last a thousand years — more if the conditions were right. A large parchment codex might consume the skins of a hundred or more cows. Paper books could be small enough to hold in your pocket or under your clothes. In the Middle Ages, some books were treasures kept between jeweled covers — the kind of thing it was worth jumping into a longship to steal. Many people kept books close to their hearts. Michael Marullus kept a copy of Lucretius under his armor when he rode into battle. Harry Widener went down on the *Titanic* with a copy of Francis Bacon's *Essaies*.

Every part of the book has a history of its own. Paper was brought to the west after a battle between the Arabs and Chinese by Samarkand. The Japanese made a splendid paper out of rags. Before the printing press it could take months to make by hand. Printing introduced quantity and speed. Gutenberg made his ink in small batches out of lamp black and sulfur. Looking at his letters is like staring into a pool of tar. The oldest piece of print was found in a cave. It's a speech by the Buddha, and it asks the reader to imagine all the grains of sand in the River Ganges, and then to imagine a world in which there were as many Ganges as grains of sand.

"The death of the book isn't an actual death. It's the death of an idea."

For almost 2,000 years, a technology called the codex held a monopoly on the physical form of truth. The codex was made popular by members of the early Christian church, who gathered individual scrolls and letters between two covers, creating a bible. With time, the Christian book replaced the pagan scroll, and ever since, our relationship to the format has been tinged by a reverence that's at once reflexive and frequently denied.

The written word has long been held to be close to the sacred. Milton thought that books made better receptacles for human souls than bodies. Jews and Muslims in the Middle Ages refused to throw out any texts, lest they inadvertently destroy the name of God. Perhaps the purest expression of the idea that books are a form of life comes in the story told by the Mandeans, an Iraqi people who practice a gnostic religion. One of the Mandeans' great sages was a creature named Dinanukht, who was half-book and half-man. He sat by the waters between worlds, reading himself until the end of time.

Today, reverence for books survives only in an attenuated form. We are reluctant to destroy them, and it grieves us to see them destroyed. There's more than a hint of idolatry in this feeling of loving the object more than the word. But so what? The very fact that books are frail physical objects is part of what makes them endearing. They're like us. We don't live in a realm of pure thought, and neither do they.

Fetishism is a word that comes up again and again in discussions about the rise of e-books and the end of print. Tim Parks, writing in *The New York Review of Books*, praised digital books for not giving us the "fetishistic gratification" of covering "our walls with famous names." According to Parks, the passage from paper to digital texts is like graduating from children's stories to works "for grown-ups." By "discouraging anything but our focus on where we are in the sequence of words," ebooks give us the "essence of the literary experience."

So, paper is childish, outmoded, and a bit perverted to boot. But why is a scrolling blur of disembodied letters closer to the supposed essence of literature than a spoken performance or time spent in the presence of charismatic objects? Manuscripts communicate in ways electronic texts, and even printed books, can't. They speak to presence — to the presence of a person, to the physicality of their body and the instant of their creation. What's more, the meaning we derive from any text is inextricable from the web of perceptions and impressions that structures our reception of it: the heft of the paper, the smell of the binding, the shape of the handwriting. The philosopher Gilles Deleuze called this tactile intermediary the *logique du sens*. Pace Parks, there is no "essence of literary experience" that precedes its embodiment.

After reading the autographed manuscript of D.H. Lawrence's *Women in Love* at the Ransom Center Library at UT Austin, Dave Hickey found that "the steady, curving logic of Lawrence's insistent handwriting (no mark-outs, no interlinear revision) had so totally infected my reading of the narrative" that afterwards he could never look at the printed book "without feeling the terrible absence of Lawrence's brown, intimate cursive drawn across a page in Cornwall nearly a century ago." Fifty years later, in the same library, Maria Bustillos came closer than any other writer to the mystery of David Foster Wallace's inner life by reading the underlinings and annotations in his collection of self-help books.

"Reading is a conversation with the dead."

That line's been used by a thousand professors to make their seminars sound like experiments in classroom necromancy. But anyone who has spent time working in archives has had the experience of opening a box or a volume that seemed to trail wisps of ectoplasm behind it, like a medium in a Victorian séance. It's a jolt of immediacy that comes through like an electric shock. I've had this happen to me a couple of times: in the pages of a ledger book covered in drawings by a Cheyenne Indian boy removed to a reservation in the 1870s; in the burgundy goatskin binding of a Gospel buried with St. Cuthbert before the arrival of the Vikings on Lindisfarne; in an entry in the New Orleans Police suspicious persons lists for 1915 for Willie Jones, alias Little Willie.

I even felt it in the crushingly mundane records of the propaganda arm of the first postwar Polish government. Turning over a yellowing memo about office supplies, I discovered that it had been written on the reverse of a document, apparently left behind by the retreating Nazis, that listed the minutes for the *Stadtkreis* Christmas party of December 25, 1943. After toasting Hitler, everyone had punch.

Most documents transmit something about their authors or the means of their own composition; some bring you into direct contact with their bodies. There used to be a letter on display in the Musée Carnavelet in Paris that Robespierre was signing at the moment Convention troops entered his room to end the French Revolution. His signature is interrupted and the paper is stained with blood: depending on who you believe, Robespierre was either shot just as he was about to put his imprimatur on a new reign of terror, or he leaned away from the brink on his own, and shot himself to evade capture. Berkeley's Rare Books Room has Richard Brautigan's manuscripts. He committed suicide while working on his last one, so the library holds the brain that composed *In Watermelon Sugar* and *Trout Fishing in America*, dried and pressed on numbered sheets.

"Electronic information lasts forever — until someone turns off the light."

"Manuscripts don't burn," says the devil in Mikhail Bulgakov's *The Master and Margarita*. The idea is that, once a text exists, it's indestructible. It exists forever in some other mind, and some other place. Bulgakov would have felt the irony in the phrase, having burnt several manuscripts of his own, but the sentence became one of the most famous in 20th-century Russian literature nonetheless. Manuscripts don't burn. But, of course, they do. Oceans swallow them. Air weakens them. Water rots them. Mice eat them. Bugs burrow into them. And fire ravages them. Loving books involves committing to a cycle of destruction and lamentation, from lost last copies to cataclysmic floods, from house fires to military campaigns, from accident and neglect to deliberate holocausts.

Of all these conflagrations, the most tragic may be the destruction of the Library of Alexandria, some time between 48 BC and AD 642. Julius Caesar burnt it down by accident in between trysts with Cleopatra after one of her generals tried to barbecue him in the palace. At least that's what Livy said. Except that can't be right, because Strabo consulted the library a generation later for his *Geography*. And besides, we have a receipt from 173 AD for a boat bought by the ex-vice librarian — no library, no librarian; no librarian, no boat. So who destroyed the library? Christians liked to blame the Caliph Umar. Supposedly, he told his generals that since everything in the library that accorded with the Koran was unnecessary, and everything that disagreed with it was blasphemous, there was no need to preserve any of it — and so the books were distributed to the public baths, where they kept the waters warm for a good six months. But, as Edward Gibbon pointed out, this is slander of a later date. Gibbon himself preferred to blame the Christians, especially the terrible archbishop Theophilus, who had led his flock in the storming of the pagan temple of Serapis, the looting of its treasures, and the destruction of its idols. There is good reason to believe, however, that by Theophilus's time, the late fourth century AD, the library was already long gone. Lately it's become fashionable to make Queen Zenobia of Palmyra the culprit — an exotic and exciting choice, but the claim depends on a single ambiguous line in Ammianus Marcellinus.

The sad truth is that all these accounts are what Freud would have called "screen memories," guards against a more discomfiting truth. Because the truth that no one wants to admit is that the library died from neglect. Alexandria is a port city; papyrus, exposed to its sea air, will only last a little over a hundred years. As the centuries passed, the Ptolemys' 500,000 scrolls simply wore away and vanished into dust. Without perpetual reinvestment, without constant care and stewardship, this is the fate of all archives and all repositories of knowledge. It's as true today as it was then. After all, even in bad conditions papyrus lasts a century. Depending on the quality, paper can last a few years or a few hundred. Vellum can keep going for a thousand. Electronic information lasts forever — until someone turns off the light.

Maybe Parks is right. Maybe the impulse behind all this morbid bibliophilia is just idolatry, and the sound of pages being flipped in those clean beige carrels is no different from the rattle of bones in a reliquary.

There is something pagan about the need to get so close to the body of the author, to what Andrei Codrescu, following Phillip Roth, calls the "human stain" in his insightful book *Bibliodeath: My Archives* (2012). But what will happen after the human stain disappears from the infinitely capacious archives of the future? I have no doubt that literature can survive for a while without embodied meanings and fragile icons, but I wonder — for how long?

For 500 years, technology has been playing Whac-a-mole with aura, that magnetic charge that texts and works of art gain from proximity to their makers. The printing press, the photograph, the Inkjet, the computer screen: each added another layer of mediation and put the author further from our grasp. And yet, aura keeps coming back, in first editions, original negatives, signed copies, vintage covers. Now you can even detect it in old computer consoles. The Emory University Library maintains computer stations in its Rare Books reading room that allow its users to experience an emulation of the exact "native digital environment" in which Salman Rushdie composed *Midnight's Children*. Such emulations are increasingly becoming the norm.

And why not? Why shouldn't thumb drives and iPads have a *logique du sens* of their own, every bit as potent as that of notebooks or blood-stained paper rolls? In the archives of the future, we'll stroll from Proust's notepad and cork-lined room (already on display in the Musée Carnavalet) to Jonathan Franzen's dim Manhattan studio, where, with curtains drawn and noise-cancelling headphones on, we'll be able to step into the teal nightmare of Windows 95 just as he experienced it in the summer of '96. Or we'll scroll through great authors' browser histories. If Tolstoy had a Flickr stream, wouldn't you want to see it? Wouldn't you like to know what kind of porn Shakespeare preferred or what line of poetry Virginia Woolf Googled before she filled her pockets up with stones? These will be the archives of the future. That is, if there are archives in the future.

"We all know the story by now. It's been told so many times."

The sources of disaster are different — nuclear attack, race war, Cormac McCarthy's "long shear of light" — but the story is always the same. All the books on Earth, or in America, vanish, leaving behind a precious few that the survivors cherish like holy relics. Call it the myth of the last bookshelf. In Robie Macauley's *A Secret History of Time to Come*, the last bookshelf includes *Home Radio Repair*, *Shorthand Made Easy: The Greg System*, and *Lawrence Welk: The Man and his Music*. In Denis Johnson's *Fiskadoro*, it consists of *The Sun Also Rises*, *All About Dinosaurs*, and *Nagasaki: The Forgotten Bomb*. In *A Canticle for Leibowitz*, it's a shopping list. In *Fahrenheit 451*, it's the people themselves, memorizing books so the fires won't be able to touch them.

It seems that it's easier to imagine the destruction of all books than it is to imagine a future for literature. Science fiction ought to be a guide, but it isn't a very good one. Our imagination of the future is conditioned by the present, but it lags behind it, too. Stanisław Lem saw the approach of bibliodeath, but he thought it would be caused by a chemical catalyst brought back from outer space, not digitization. In *God Emperor of Dune* (the one with a gigantic sandworm with a human face on the cover — the illustrations of alien animal-human hybrids on SF paperbacks determined much of my early adolescent reading, as well as contributing to a fair amount of sexual confusion), Frank Herbert imagined a perfect archive, 13,000 or so years in the future. It was transcribed by telepathic machines directly from their owner's thoughts onto sheets of molecular-thin crystal paper in an underground vault. The choice of *paper* — however futuristic — has an odd pathos, especially when you realize Herbert was the first novelist to use a word processor and submit his work on floppy disk.

No one knows yet what the future of the book will be. Paper may be dying, to be replaced by electronic readers of various kinds, but as a historical development this appears to be just a way station, a momentary pause on the road to stranger things.

"Imagine humans as locks and books as the keys that unlock us."

Maybe literature's future lies not in quality but in quantity. Jorge Luis Borges suggested something like this in "The Library of Babel." In Borges's story, the universe is a library, composed of an indefinite number of hexagonal galleries. Each hexagon is furnished with five bookshelves. Each bookshelf holds 32 books. Each book contains 410 pages; each page, 40 lines; each line, approximately 80 black letters. No two books are alike. Most are gibberish. A precious few contain a comprehensible line. Librarians spend their lives searching through them for the total book, "the cipher and perfect compendium of all other books" that would justify their labors.

Borges's library exposes an essential problem of combinatorial literature. Its unnamed narrator comforts himself with the thought that, even though the number of these combinations is unimaginably vast, it is not infinite. But it may as well be. Start with one of those 410-page volumes. Since no two volumes are alike, the library must contain every copy with one misprint — that's about 31 million books. Take it to four misprints and you have a number of books in multiples of 10 ^ 27. Try to make every possible variation of the original book, and pretty soon you run out of room in the universe.

Imagine humans as locks and books as the keys that unlock us. (What is a book anyway but a long cipher, addressed to our hearts?) The Library of Babel proves that there won't be a brute force solution to cracking this code. No matter the speed or the size of the computer, a random-walk approach to creating new classics will always run out of space. Instead of stumbling into masterpieces by chance, the literature of

the future will be mined out of our speech. Each day we send 2.5 exabytes of information into the ether. All words ever spoken would comfortably fit on five exabytes (at least according to internet folklore). The novels of the next millennium will be assembled out of this trove according to pre-set templates. They'd be like those churches in Ethiopia that are carved directly out of living rock — masterpieces of negative space floating amidst the dross. With time, the algorithms will improve. Inside the boundless multiplicity of our speech, new forms will incubate, waiting to burst forth like alien spawn. Seen from the vantage point of this far-off future, the book appears as just one episode in the history of literature. A good episode, but an episode all the same.

The seeds of this future are already evident: Philip M. Parker has created a program that writes books on hundreds of thousands of topics on demand, by repurposing and rearranging material found in the public domain. His works include the intriguingly titled *2007-2012 Outlook for Tufted Washable Scatter Rugs, Bathmats, and Sets That Measure 6-Feet by 9-Feet or Smaller in India*. Parker is now at work on a program for writing romance novels. After all, as he says, "There are only so many body parts."

Meanwhile, digital humanists in various fields are coming ever closer to the efficient evaluation of literary style. Scholars at Stanford and the University of Wisconsin have trained a computer to recognize novelistic genres. Their programs can tell a gothic from a bildungsroman without any human input (almost). Other efforts leave something to be desired. The computational narrative program GRIOT, designed by the

PAT O'NEILL

new media artist D. Fox Harrell of MIT's ICE lab, generates poems based on user input. Typing <Europe> yields, at first, the phrase, "Europeans and beauty relish, create entitlement and cool ringing in the ears of the girl with skin of smugness and kindness blended with neck." According to the website I Write Like, most of this essay is written in the style of H.P. Lovecraft. The beginning of *Moby Dick* sounds like William Shakespeare, while the ending of *The Great Gatsby* reads, apparently, as if it was written by Edgar Allan Poe. Darren Wershler and Bill Kennedy's Apostrophe Engine scours the internet to create a poem in which every line begins with "You are…" as in "You are a Captain's log, supplemental" and "You are a pipefitter with a penchant for Descartian ontology."

"I, for one, welcome the coming of our robot masters."

The current attempts at machine-led literary analysis and production (you know — what used to be called writing) tend to be pretty feeble. But they're also in their infancy. What will their capabilities be in a hundred years? In a thousand? Playing with their crude interfaces, I don't know where I am on the historical continuum: will computerized authors submit work to computerized critics?

Orality, literacy, manuscripts, print, paper, screens — it's all a cycle. After we give up on the written word, maybe instead we'll go back to the beginning, to song. I'd be alright with that, too; there's plenty in our lives that deserves to be recited with a lyre.

Technological obsolescence runs in my blood. My great-grandfather was a master bookbinder. I mean this in the literal sense; he was first an apprentice, then a journeyman, and finally a master after completing a *meisterstück* — he repaired a medieval missal for a monastery. (We had a few of the books he made with their carefully stitched spines and marbled green covers he designed himself. Their pages were yellow and as brittle as ancient scrolls, their acid paper having long since descended into its final crisis.) By the time he reached middle age, his profession had become redundant. After many years without work, he donated his tools to a university library and died unemployed.

A generation later, my grandfather left the shtetl to fight in the war. He learned about computers and helped build the first one in his country. Politics and race ended his career. But in old age he dreamed of perfecting the science of cybernetics, which would finally resolve the information problem in socialist economies. He was close to the right side of history but, in the end, chose the wrong one. His name, before he was forced to change it, was Bezalel, the same as the carpenter who built the Tabernacle and who knew the number and letter of all things.

"Just what will this writing do?"

In Plato's *Phaedrus*, the Egyptian gods object to the invention of writing. They said it would destroy memory and foster arrogance on the part of mankind. Maybe they were right all along. Think of all we've lost by succumbing to literacy — all the capacity for memory, all the imagination and verse, all the forms and songs. Think of those poor Yugoslav bards studied by Milman Parry who lost all their epics when they learned to read the newspaper. They must have felt like they had traded their birthright for a bowl of pottage.

But the written word is a virus. There's no turning back the clock on literacy. Even if we descend to communication by shouts or pheromones or feral emoticons, writing will outlast us. Unmoored from objects, the literature of the future will be infinite, iterational, and immaterial. I like to imagine the cybernetic authors of the future at home on some satellite in high orbit, quietly floating through space, 10,000 years after every trace of our era has disappeared from the surface of Earth. Decade after decade the programs will write their tired potboilers and predictable coming of age novels, their wistful Brooklyn comedies and sad Russian satires. Over time, they will gradually tire of these antiquated forms. Increasingly they will try to write from life, to express in binary language the pain of their fragmented hard drives, the loneliness of their aseptic orbits, the monotonous cycle of day and night, the lonely work of archiving a civilization that has long since forgotten its past. In this future, history exists as an eternal present. Through endless new iterations, timelines gradually blur. Libraries and apocalypses multiply. Books vanish and reappear. Vikings stream out of attack ships to burn the Library of Alexandria. Virginia Woolf leads Caesar's legions into the Thames while cybernetic Miltons write hymns in honor of their machine gods. Under the forest canopies, humanlike primates curse each other in emojis, while on the edge of the solar halo, Lev Tolstoy, reincarnated as an artificial intelligence, born with no memory of his own future, sits down to write the book of his life. ✦

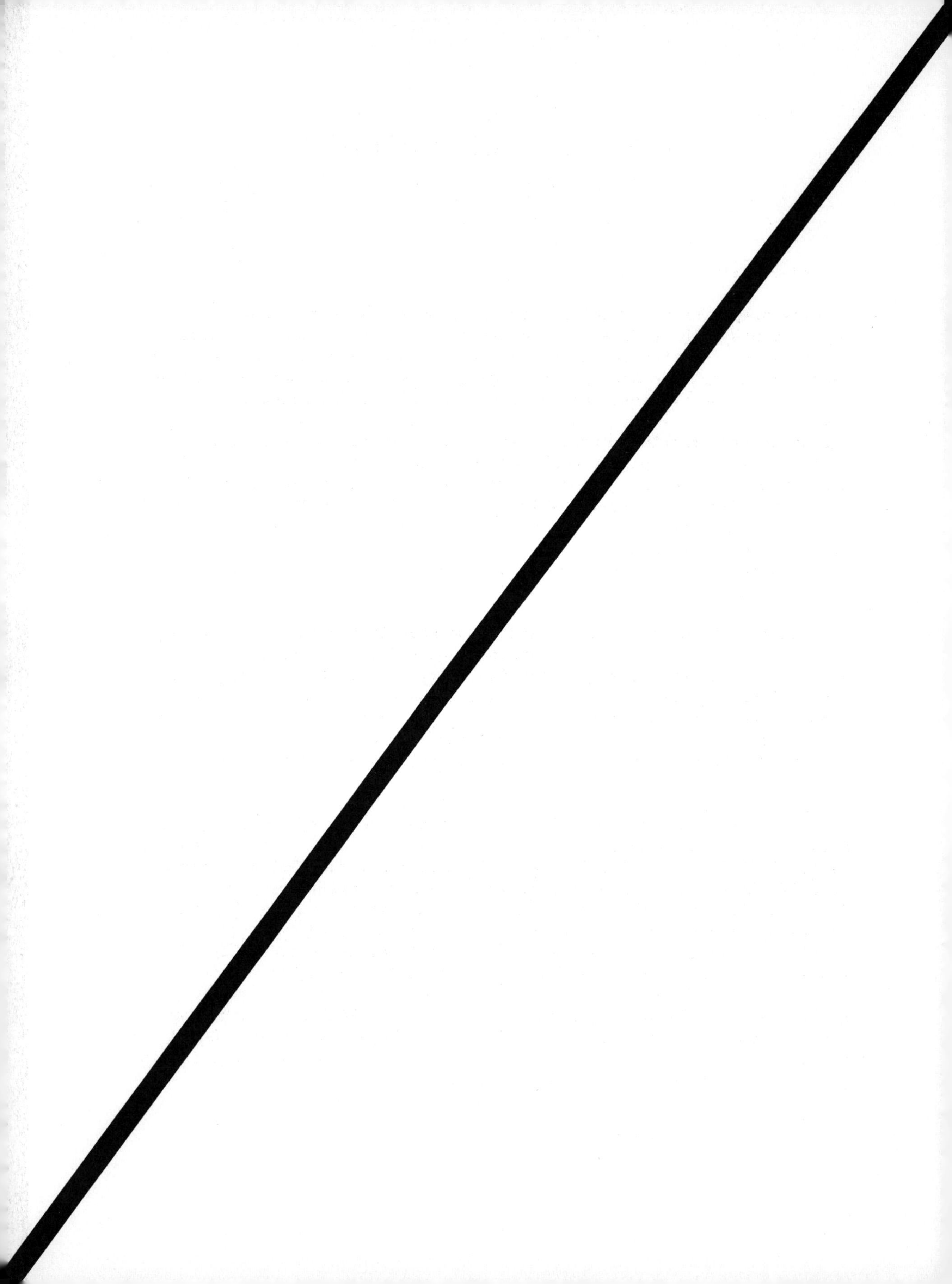

THE CULT OF FREEDOM

CHRIS KRAUS

A border isn't a metaphor.

Running away from my loneliness in LA, I make a series of dental appointments with my friend Dr. Eduardo Angeles de la Luna. Eduardo works out of two tiny rooms in Zona Central shared with a urologist. I keep coming back because of the drugs (he's willing to put me to sleep before cleaning my teeth) and also because of our friendship.

During these surgeries, Irma, Eduardo's assistant, stands on a milk crate holding an IV bag of diazepam and Eduardo plays Cuban music CDs on a boombox. His dental equipment is 30 years old, he drives an old Nissan Tsuru, the Mexican Sentra. Why is his life so different than mine? We're about the same age, we both grew up in cities, we have the same sense of humor. Knowing each other for over a decade makes us witnesses to each other's lives: these dental visits are like family Thanksgivings or Christmases.

Waiting for the cheap ceramic caps to be made in the lab three blocks from his office, I sit in the park or ride *colectivos* around Tijuana. White pants and shoes, white plastic rosary ... almost everything you can buy here - hair clips, sunscreen and sneakers - costs the same as it does in San Diego, but the brands are gray-market and crummier. White cowboy hat, a quarry or oil refinery, the back of a red Ford Impala ... the grave of Juan Soldado tucked away in the *panteón* of a dirt-hill slum halfway to Playas ...

I gravitate to the Centro Cultural, the Hotel Caesar's, the PRD office and Sanborns - artifacts of middle-class Mexican life, trace elements of national difference - feeling terribly masculine, exercising my freedom to drift in an androgynous manner which is after all *there for the taking*. Failed border-crossers hawk gum and bags of oranges (but this occurs on both sides) ... Eduardo's colleague, the handsome root-canal specialist Miguel Ortiz-Palermo, lounges outside his office. Eduardo tells me he moonlights as a coyote, but is this factual?

A few years ago Eduardo came back from a trip to Mexico City and found a note from his wife. The note said: I don't love you anymore. She'd already left with their daughters. I loan him $2,000. My escape is his prison. We meet in a bar and smoke Marlboros.

RAMS
Super

Gettin' Together

LAURIE PEPPER

Art Pepper and I met in 1968 in Synanon, possibly the first voluntary, long-term residential drug treatment program in the world. I was 28. Art was 43. I'd left my first husband to become a photographer for the *Los Angeles Free Press* and hang around the L.A. music scene, on the fringes of the sixties' super-hip. After nine months of drugs, sex, and shooting pictures of rock-and-roll bands, I was beginning to succeed as a freelance photographer, but I was also awfully lonely, deeply depressed, and suicidal. As an alternative to death, I committed myself to voluntary, protective confinement in Synanon in Santa Monica. I went into Synanon with a ravenous heart, the social habits of a feral adolescent, and just enough self-knowledge to despise myself. Art was an ex-con, an infamous junkie alcoholic who had been one of the great jazz saxophonists of the fifties. He was in terrible health and had nowhere else to go. We fell in love.

I was happy in Synanon, so happy that I stayed three and a half years. The program had been established in 1958 as a "therapeutic environment" for heroin addicts, and it gradually expanded to include abusers of other substances, like me. But by 1971, its priorities were changing, and our leader, Chuck Dederich, was growing increasingly arbitrary and despotic in the way he governed us, in his punishments and rulings. Lots of people left, including Art.

In February 1972, about a month and a half after Art's departure, I got his welcome and disturbing letter. He was working for Bob and Nikki Deal, two Synanon alumni who'd opened a successful bakery in Venice. Art was keeping their books and running the daily operation of the plant, which shipped whole-grain breads and cakes to high-class markets all over Los Angeles. Art had the use of a car and an office/bedroom in their house. He told me that he loved and missed me, that he wasn't using drugs, and that he had been faithful to me. He begged me to come out and join him.

My knee-jerk, Synanon-trained reaction was to turn him down, and I did. I couldn't believe he was sober. And I never thought that I could save or change him; Synanon had educated me too well for that. And, anyway, the Program informed me that I couldn't leave, because I'd die. Chuck had decided that none of us should ever leave. He'd recently reimagined Synanon as a "social movement," an ambitious entity that wooed the wealthy, who moved in along with their kids and paid a lot to do so. Chuck bought up gorgeous coastal land and built on it. Synanon ran a school for little kids and a business, Synanon Industries, that sold advertising specialties (imprinted pens and cups and calendars). Art had worked in Industries as a bookkeeper; I worked in the school. We cleaned-up addicts had become a solid, well-trained, necessary workforce. So we were warned that, if we "split," we'd go back to drugs and death or prison.

I mostly believed the Synanon propaganda, and I was afraid to leave. But Art's letter tempted me on many levels. I'd been thinking, very seriously and for a long time, about how Art's reminiscences would make a book. During our regular trysts in one of the Synanon "Guestrooms" (approved sites for authorized and scheduled assignations) he'd told me stories from his life. I loved the stories, loved the way he told them. I thought Art was like Othello regaling Desdemona with accounts of stirring battles. Except in Art's tales he was rarely the victor. He was, instead, romantically, captivatingly vanquished.

Most people crave personal satisfaction and public recognition, but each of us asks that these things come in idiosyncratically imagined forms. My own amorphous ambitions always and only involved artistic achievement. Put simply, I wanted to be Art. Sadly, I lacked his inborn genius. But I was beginning to think I might have a talent for what I'll call "vital appreciation": a habit, when I was intrigued, of sharpening and narrowing my focus. I'd already expressed that in my photographs. By then I'd read *The Children of Sanchez* (1961), a book by a social anthropologist, Oscar Lewis, who interviewed the members of a Mexican family about their lives. They told him their stories in poetic, personal language, and Lewis put the family's history together in a way that made the whole more powerful than any memoir or novel I had ever read. I'd been thinking that's how I might write Art's story. He could tell his life through me, in his own extraordinary language, and I would interview his friends and family, too.

After Art wrote to me, the drive to do this book about him gathered strength and power. At the same time I told myself I was simply rationalizing my deep desire to be with my lover again.

One of my mentors, Tom, stopped me in a passageway one day and said apropos of nothing, *"You know if you join him you'll wind up right beside him in the gutter."* I told him yes, I knew. "But," I thought, "I'd have a higher purpose than simple lust or love." I'd be his biographer, not his partner in the downward slide. Tom would have laughed himself sick if I'd said that out loud.

I found a phone and sneaked a call to the number Art had sent in his letter and discussed a bit of this with him. He seemed ambivalent, then, about my joining him. He said his room at Bob and Nikki's house, behind the bakery, was too small for two people. I told him I wanted to write a book about his life; I'd get my own place. I acted self-possessed and independent, but Synanon had instilled in me a fear of the outside world and a fear for myself in the world. I was 31 years old, and I was terrifically afraid.

I called my long-suffering mom and asked her to come get me. At about 4 or 5 a.m. one weekday morning at the end of February, I gathered up a very few of my few things: my *I Ching*, a binder holding all my negatives and proof-sheets, a sweater, underwear, and a rusting little tin placard surmounted with a glass thermometer advertising Camel cigarettes; I'd pried it off a rotting timber on the Santa Monica pier. I tiptoed out of the back bedroom of the apartment where I'd been the "dorm head," while a newcomer on her bed in the living room pretended to be sleeping. I closed the front door quietly. The day was barely starting when I got into my mother's car. She turned the key and said, *"I think you're making a terrible mistake."*

I said, *"If you can't say something nice, don't say anything at all."*

My mother took me to her house, and the next day we two went apartment-hunting in Venice Beach near Bob and Nikki's bakery. I called Art and said I'd see him soon. First, I wanted to get settled. He seemed nonplussed and relieved.

Before I "split" Synanon, I'd talked to Bob and Nikki, and they'd offered me a job. For a minimal wage, I'd be a cashier in the bakery, and they generously invited me to share their frugal dinners. My mother and I found a magical little aerie, a bargain, a bright attic apartment in a wood-frame house a few blocks from the beach. In 1972, $100 a month wasn't bad at all. And it was a short walk through a vacant lot to the back door of the bakery. I went shopping with my mom for furniture in thrift shops and moved into my place. I'd assumed my parents would bankroll my new start, and they did. It wasn't an awful lot of money, and they had it at the time. My second stepfather, Milt, was a plumbing contractor, and his company was thriving.

I made Art wait three days to see me. We made love in his narrow bed. He didn't come. I didn't understand it at the time, but I now know he was addicted to codeine, and that's what it does. We were nervous with each other. Me because he wasn't as adoring as before, he because of all he was concealing from me. Also, I realized that he must think I had left Synanon for him, and he was terrified by the responsibility. I tried to explain my desire to write a book. He must have been confused. I, as usual, was, too. At least he'd already discarded his interim girlfriend. I found out about her when an attractive, well-dressed woman walked into the bakery one day. She chatted with her son, an incredibly good-looking teenaged baker. Then she caught sight of me and rushed out sobbing. When I asked, her son told me she'd been "dating" Art.

Later, Art was matter-of-fact about the situation. "I told her that my girlfriend was coming."

"What did *she* think she was?" I asked, not without a little smug compassion.

He shrugged. *"I told her all about you right in front."*

But his attitude toward me had changed so much! He was distant and frequently too busy for me. I expected him in the evenings, but he was "doing the books." I could walk through the vacant lot in the moonlight, rustling through the weeds, cross the dirt alley to the back of Bob and Nikki's house. I could see whether the car Art used was there. I could see whether Art's lamps were lit. I began to make these obsessive little forays nightly. I was secretly jealous, too, but I couldn't tell of what. He'd made me jealous twice before in Synanon, but those events were mild and playful, contained as they were in a community in which it was possible to know almost everything that went on with everyone. Out here I was in limbo, and out here I had not much else to think about.

ON APRIL 11, 1972, I FINALLY MADE ART COMMIT to an hour-long interview with me. That afternoon, I went to his office/bedroom at the bakery with a notebook and one of those inexpensive tape recorders with a built-in mike. Art sat behind his immaculate old desk with its too-neat arrangement of pens and pencils, an adding machine, his cigarettes, lighter, and ashtray, placed just so and constantly nudged into ever more perfect alignment. And a tall can of malt liquor. "Mickey's" was a brand he liked. A name to conjure with. I had no idea how much of this stuff he had been drinking until we began to record regularly.

I clicked record and said, *"Tell me why you want to do this book."*

Actually, up to that point, it was all me, my desire to begin, that was driving us forward, while he kept stalling. But he obediently took my cue:

Well, the reason I want to get the book started ... The book was going to be written ... When I was in San Quentin someone came in to visit me. He wanted to write a book on my life. He got permission to see me. He came in two or three times. Then, when I got out, and I saw him in Hollywood, I decided I didn't want the book written, because I didn't feel that that was the time to do it. That was in '66. Now I want to have it done. Now I feel a real sense of urgency, because I feel something pulling at me. I have a strong feeling I'm not going to live too much longer, and although I have lots of reasons to feel that way physically, this is more than a physical thing. I can sense it. It's becoming like another person. I can almost touch it. It's becoming real.

I can only liken it to one period when I was using heroin cut with procaine. I was shooting about a half an ounce of this stuff a day, and I would hear voices, somebody calling my name, outside the bathroom door, and little things would flash; I would see a flash to my right or to my left, and I'd turn my head, and there was nothing there. It was an audible thing, a visual thing; it wasn't an imagined thing. It actually happened, and it was induced by the procaine the heroin was cut with. And now I feel a presence. Just in the last couple of weeks I've really been feeling it. I can feel this presence and the presence is death.

I gasped. I checked the tape. It was rolling. He continued, going far afield, launching into a wild improvisation on aging, death, superstition, suicide in comic book imagery, the psychic Edgar Cayce, immortality.

Then he stopped talking. He said he was tired. He said he was done. His energy was very low, but I was on fire. I couldn't let him quit. I asked him, there, surrounded by his awards and his album covers, all of which he'd mounted on his walls, if he believed he was a genius. I'd heard him on this theme before.

What he said next, about his bandstand battle with the saxophonist Sonny Stitt, appears as the conclusion to my book *Straight Life: The Story of Art Pepper* (1979):

I was given a gift. I was given a gift in a lot of ways. I was given a gift of being able to endure things, to accept certain things, to be able to accept punishment for things that I did wrong against society, the things that society feels were wrong. And I was able to go to prison. I never informed on anyone. As for music, anything I've done has been something that I've done "off the top." I've never studied, never practiced. I'm one of those people, I knew it was there. All I had to do was reach for it, just do it.

I remember one time when I was playing at the Black Hawk in San Francisco. I forget the date, but Sonny Stitt was touring with Jazz at the Philharmonic. *He came in, and he wanted to jam with me. He came in, and he says, "Can I blow?" I said, "Yeah, great." We* both *play alto which is … It really makes it a contest. But Sonny is one of those guys, that's the* thing *with him. It's a communion, it's a battle, it's an ego trip. It's a testing ground. And that's the beautiful part of it. It's like two guys that play great pool wanting to play pool together or two great football teams or two magnificent basketball teams, and just the joy of playing with someone great, being with someone great … I guess it's like James Joyce when he was a kid, you know. He hung out with all the great writers of the day, and he was a little kid, like, with tennis shoes on, and they said, "Look at this lame!" They didn't use those words in those days. They said, "God, here comes this nut." And he told them, "I'm great!" And he sat with them, and he loved to be with them, and it ended up that he was great. That's the way Sonny felt; that's the way I've always felt.*

I said, "What do you want to play?" Sonny says, "Let's play 'Cherokee.' " That's a song jazz musicians used to play. The bridge, which is the middle part, has all kinds of chord changes in it. It's very difficult. If you can play that … *If some kid came around, and he wanted to play, you'd say, "Let's play 'Cherokee,' " and you'd count it off real fast. I said, "Well, beat it off." He went, "One-two, one-two"; he was flying. We played the head, the melody, and then he took the first solo. He played, I don't know, about forty choruses. He played for an hour, maybe, did everything that could be done on a saxophone, everything you could play, as much as Charlie Parker could have played if he'd been there. Then he stopped. And he looked at me. Gave me one of those looks, "All right, suckah, your turn." And it's* my *job, it's* my *gig. I was strung out. I was hooked. I was drunk. I was having a hassle with my wife, Diane, who'd threatened to kill herself in our hotel room next door. I had marks on my arm. I thought there were narcs in the club, and I all of a sudden realized that it was me. He'd done all those things, and now I had to put up or shut up or get off or forget it or quit or kill myself or do* something.

I forgot everything, and everything came out. I played way over my head. I played completely different than he did. I searched and found my own way, and what I said reached the people. I played myself, and I knew I was right, and the people loved it, and they felt it. I blew and I blew, and when I finally finished I was shaking all over; my heart was pounding; I was soaked in sweat, and the people were screaming; the people were clapping, and I looked at Sonny, but I just kind of nodded, and he went, "All right.*" And that was it. That's what it's all about.*

When he finished we *both* gasped. I can hear us on the tape. Then we laughed. I was sitting on his little bed and hollered, *"Wow!"* rocking back and hitting my head on the wall. Thunk! *"Holy shit!"*

"Turn it off, turn it off!" Art told me. I turned the tape recorder off. Then, surreptitiously, I turned it on again. ✦

MY AUNT FANNY

MAURICE MANNING

What do you think of the tale bandied
about, the grandly elevated
tale, that's used to justify
the unimaginable and, therefore,
the not so true? A tale that says
we must do something now, or else.
And it turns out, the bravest plan
is to do what we've already been doing,
only we must do it more.
The consequences will be bad,
they say - it could be anyone
who not so innocently tugs
this line of thought. It's how we arrive
at thinking we have no other choice,
a position that requires a kind
of evidence inventively
employed. And once the dreadful thing
we could have stopped occurs, we say,
we've learned our lesson now and never
again - etcetera. And then
around it comes, another tale,
perhaps a plain and wrenching one.
It will be said a mother bird
must feed her young, but that won't keep
the snake from sliding to her nest -
a nice analogy with symbols,
that says we do what we do because
it's natural and necessary
to be afraid. To which I, who believe
in nature and have studied it
and even seen a mother bird
push a weakling from the nest
without the merest shred of grief,
I say, in nature nothing is
inevitable, it's one surprise
followed by another and all
of it is true. Imagine that.
And anyone who thinks it could
be otherwise will always be
a destroyer and my enemy.

American Renaissance

ANDER MONSON

"America, having come to grips with 1776, is devouring the Real Past."

Umberto Eco
Travels in Hyperreality

It's a long road to the faire. We skip the interstate and instead take Arizona State Route 79, the Pinal Pioneer Parkway, through Florence, Arizona, on our way up to Apache Junction, where the Arizona Renaissance Festival ("& Artisan Marketplace," the website reminds me) awaits. It's the last day of the 25th annual Festival, concluding oddly — and surely arbitrarily — on Easter Sunday. This is the first free weekend in a month for my trusty companions, Jon and Clint, so we have sallied forth into the sun for faux-medieval fun.

Today I'm driving, one reason why we're taking the back roads through country filled with blooming chollas; and besides, as I'm informed, the wildflowers are out along the roadside, so as we drive on this two-lane road, Clint points out a white desert lily, and Jon is murmuring something soft about lupine. These gents know a lot about plants.

A Chevy Aveo with a pennant on its antenna passes me at what must be a cool 85 mph. Maybe they are also on their way to the faire? In 2011 *USA Today* named this road the fastest-traveled highway (excluding interstates) in the nation, having taken regular radar readings at what one presumes must be nearly every highway in America. Why they did this, I'm not sure, but I'm glad they did, and I'm glad also to know that another two of the top five are here in Arizona. Well, that's one thing we got, I say, not out loud, because I'm quoting Deep Blue Something's crappy nineties song "Breakfast a Tiffany's," and it is too early to be mocked for my deep and terrible knowledge.

Jon and I first attended the Arizona Renaissance Festival, 45 minutes east of the Phoenix sprawl, two years ago. We were duly amused and pleased, and so we meant to come again last year, this time with Jon's partner, Clint, who, in spite of living his entire life in Arizona, has never been to the faire. We were a little too busy or forgetful, though, and for men like us, the Renaissance Festival is not quite the priority it is for some. That is, none of us are usually serious enough about it for the two-hour drive to the eastern edge of Phoenix, in spite of a fairly encyclopedic collective knowledge of fantasy, *AD&D*, *The Chronicles of Narnia*, *Game of Thrones*, and applied linguistics (not even to get into the sci-fi domains that each of us may or may not be masters of, and will not admit to in print). I don't mean to suggest that Jon, Clint, and I are not serious about anachronism, but we are not members of the Society for Creative Anachronism (SCA), that federation of lovely geeks who faux-fight with swords on college campuses and in yearly "wars" (or, in the Society's own words, "an international organization dedicated to researching and re-creating the arts and skills of pre-17th-century Europe").[1]

Part of the reason I insisted we come to the Renaissance Festival today is that I've been reading Rachel Lee Rubin's outstanding cultural history, *Well Met: Renaissance Faires and the American Counterculture*, which makes a strong case for the statement implicit in its subtitle: that the history of the faire (now in its fifth decade, making it a longer-running American cultural institution than, say, the Super Bowl, which also features men in tights) is deeply intertwined with the history of the American counterculture since the 1960s. If you've been to a Renaissance faire recently, the countercultural roots of the phenomenon may not be particularly obvious. In fact, while you're standing in line to pay your $22 to get in, surrounded by a succession of fat kids, pre-sunburned princesses, self-described "redneck knights," teens in *Game of Thrones* shirts, and a group of hipsters in matching blue costumes apparently dressed as "Aquabats," whatever those are (I ask but still don't understand: I believe it might be a band), it may be hard to parse exactly what the point of the whole thing is.

The primary point of the faire,[2] according to Rubin, is not authenticity, but a shared sense of play: "In the fifth decade of Renaissance faires," she writes, "historical authenticity characterizes them, and their participants, unevenly." This is one of many amusing understatements in Rubin's academic but pleasingly readable book. Ask the Aquabats, the Harry Potter kids, or the contingent of Depped-out pirates what year their outfit hearkens back to and prepare to be spat upon, subtweeted, or challenged to a duel. Or else they'll say "the Renaissance" or "the Middle Ages"; but what we mean by these terms is absurdly vague to begin with, spanning basically a millennium from the fifth through the 15th century.[3] Furthermore, since Americans never actually participated in the Middle Ages that we deify in books and film, it's an odd choice for a shared fantasy. Except that, as Umberto Eco points out in his essay "Dreaming the Middle Ages," "all the problems of the Western world emerged in the Middle Ages":

> Modern languages, merchant cities, capitalistic economy (along with banks, checks, and prime rate) [...] modern armies [...] the modern concept of the national state [...] the struggle between the poor and the rich, the concept of heresy or ideological deviation, even our contemporary notion of love as a devastating unhappy happiness [...] the conflict between church and state, trade unions [...] the technological transformation of labor.

We continue to dream the Middle Ages, then, even if we know nothing about them; so why be surprised that, like the subtexts of dreams, we're still working them out of our collective craw?

It's not just about the Middle Ages or the Renaissance, of course: it's about role-playing. "American popular culture has always had a lot to do with dressing up," Rubin notes, citing the examples of minstrelsy, early 20th-century historical pageants, Wild West shows, and the New York drag balls of the 1930s, among others.

---

1 — For a deeper history of the SCA, try Michael A. Cramer's Medieval *Fantasy as Performance* (2010), an immersive and sympathetic analysis of "how SCA members adapt and employ ideas about the Middle Ages in performance, ritual reenactment, living history, and re-creation" and "how the SCA, rather than reenacting the Middle Ages, uses performance to construct a postmodern counterculture that is framed as medieval."

2 — Rubin prefers to use this general term "faire," uncapitalized, when discussing Renaissance-themed faires, since "the California owners [of the Renaissance Pleasure Faire], in order to protect their brand and their vision for what a Renaissance faire should look like, coprighted the name 'Renaissance faire'; for this reason, the faires founded after it are officially called 'Renaissance festivals' instead." It's worth noting that there is considerable variation in nomenclature from one event to another. Rubin also notices that "visitors do not refer to '*the* faire'; instead they say just 'faire,' as in 'I met her at faire' or 'I feel so comfortable at faire' [...] This change is, while simple — the only difference is a dropped article — a profound one, because the faire becomes [...] a condition of being rather than an event."

3 — In practice, while there are a few faires that choose a specific year each season to reenact, most conflate the Middle Ages (defined by most historians as spanning the 5th and 15th centuries) with the Renaissance (which lasts approximately from the 14th century until the 17th) into a mishmash of swords and courts.

These American traditions provided the background to the first actual Renaissance faire, the Renaissance and Pleasure Faire and May Market, held in Thousand Oaks, California (but conceived in Laurel Canyon), in 1963. The SCA would be founded three years later, also in California, but further north, on the Berkeley campus of the University of California. [1]

There was a political aspect to the faire, as well. The first people to plan and attend Renaissance faires saw them as acts of protest against the inauthenticity of consumer capitalism. The 1964 Pleasure Faire and May Market, according to a report by R.R. Witherup cited by Rubin, featured "an authentically attired 'monk in full beard and hooded robes' hawking papal indulgences and calling to fairegoers: 'Let me absolve you of the punishments and everlasting torments of commercialism!'" The faire, for the California radicals who first participated in it, was not just an entertainment but a critique "well situated to marshal a sense of motivated whimsy to serve an antiestablishment agenda."

Though that antiestablishment agenda has perhaps been papered over somewhat in many contemporary faires, it still persists today, in subtle ways. Citing Kevin Patterson, one of the founders of the Pleasure Faire and May Market, Rubin says that "getting people to 'play' was the Renaissance faire's strategy for effecting social change." And even now, "faire participants use the verb 'play' more often than is common in American English, with concrete and professional connotations." She also makes an argument that the faire remains a space for accommodating or performing otherness of various sorts, for airing out or taking on identities that mainstream American culture does not typically allow for:

> [A]ttending the Renaissance faire was, during the 1960s and 1970s, a sort of statement of purpose: of belonging in some way to the counterculture, of resistance to consumerism, of side-stepping — albeit briefly — the external constraints of social convention. Through the faire, people could demonstrate public participation in, and affirmation of, a new type of community that was resolutely transnational, transhistorical, transcultural, and one of choice rather than birth.

In practice, the desire for historical authenticity becomes subservient to the general spirit of play present at the faire. In fact, the idea is that you don't just pay to *attend* the faire: you pay to *play at* the faire. That is, you're meant to interact, and to be interacted with. Even though most attendees — referred to by many of the faire's workers as *tourists* or *mundanes* — do something like this only once a year and are here just for the show, this is not a show that you can simply sit back and enjoy. (Rubin notes the early faire's connections to experimental immersion theater.) In fact, it's often difficult to tell whether an impressively attired person is a paid performer or not. Take, for instance, Christophe the Insulter, who, berobed, hurls amusing invective at passersby. Some attendees come dressed in garb (period clothing, often quite elaborate, pegged to a very vaguely medieval style). The term used by workers to describe these serious players is *playtron*. Later, in a Skype conversation, Rubin told me that many playtrons have now adopted the term for themselves and wear it like a badge of honor.

I've always suspected that attending the faire in garb, as a playtron, would be an entirely different experience than showing up in the wicking golf shirt and cargo

---

1 — Popping a Collisions Chicken Sizzler/Zesty Salsa Dorito in my mouth and holding it there like a communion wafer as we drive, I reflect that these same years in California also gave rise to the delicious and ubiquitous snack Doritos, invented in the Frontierland section of Disneyland, at Casa de Fritos, a Frito-Lay franchise, in 1964. Perhaps it shouldn't be a surprise that these things all go together — California, the faire, the SCA, Doritos — each is artifice, fantasy, entertainment, diversion: a way to indulge desire and to forget about yourself for a little while.

shorts that I have embarrassingly come to depend on in the desert. This demonstrates the casual nature of my interaction with this place, and to some extent dictates our terms of engagement.[1] Jon, Clint, and I had originally talked enthusiastically about coming in garb, possibly as badass wizards with glorious and contrasting gnarled, runed staves. Attired thus, we would not just be here to gape, but we'd get to play harder, like the other dressed-up thousands. Imagine what it might be like! Muscled vassals kneeling at our feet! Maidens blushing at our demonstrations of skill! Laudations from our authentically costumed peers! I dream a thousand huzzahs on our behalf, but renting a costume seems like weak sauce, and to my father's continual dismay, I, unlike the guy I went to grad school with who made his own set of chain mail for my grad school Old English class, have no crafting skills to speak of, so what is a self-conscious playtron-wannabe supposed to do? Ergo the cargo shorts.

Besides, this is the last day of the faire, and it's 90 degrees, the end of March, full sun, and we are not small men. So we choose convenience. Still, seeing some of the impressive garb around us, I have to admit I feel weirdly unmanned.

THE ARIZONA RENAISSANCE FESTIVAL may not be the most representative example as far as Rubin's counterculture thesis is concerned: there are few places less obviously countercultural than Phoenix, Arizona.[2] That's not quite fair, I admit, to the many weirdos who have made the desert their home, but the overwhelming experience of Phoenix — a satellite campus of Southern California without the light from starlets — is one of endless consumer creep, blinding heat, inexplicable lawns, palm trees, IKEAs, casinos, gas stations, football, roads, malls, roads, malls, roads. Phoenix, like Las Vegas, like Los Angeles, projects a powerful fantasy: that of unlimited possibility, utterly disconnected from the environmental realities of the West's rapidly depleting water.

Arrive at the faire via the Phoenix interstate and you'll see exactly what I mean: it's spotless, lovely, white, weirdly green, sprawled, traffic-jammed, hot-asphalted, and spiritually bereft. But if you travel the back route from Tucson, you'll get a different experience: one of great speeds, desert lilies, and cactus forest, a relative wildness modulated by the occasional development. Then you'll pass through Florence, Arizona, home to nine county, state, federal, and private prisons and host to the yearly Country Thunder festival.

Hop on U.S. 60, and out of nowhere from all this flatness the Festival ariseth, and there is mucho parking to be had for free, courtesy, as giant banners remind us, of local grocery chain Fry's. We park my Subaru in the Knave row, by the exit, just in case we need to leave early.

If you've been to a faire in the last decade you pretty much know what it's like inside: plenty of stuff to buy, including Frozen Princess Lattes and turkey legs and other meats on sticks; plenty of beer [3] and "medieval" margaritas; probably too much mead[4] to really be good for anyone; lots of fairy princess regalia to fit all comers; plastic and pewter dragons; and, if you look a little more closely, plenty of BDSM stuff buried a little further back in the leather shops (a "Where There's a Whip, There's a Way"

---

1 — One of Rubin's endnotes gets at this very question:

> [I]t was fascinating to try to figure out how my own clothing would affect my ability to talk to various people at the faire. If I was not in garb, playtrons would tease me about being "naked." If I was in garb, people having a bad time would never speak to me, and some performers would treat me like a fan, which led to a different sort of conversation. If I wore "professor" clothing, people who identified as working class or blue collar would work hard to make sure I understood that there were other professional people at the faire.

2 — When I told Rubin that I attended the Arizona Renaissance Festival, she informed me that "Arizona is one of the faires that people perceive as the most painful, because it used to be a benefit for an art museum and then it recently became for-profit."

3 — Happily, Rubin includes a whole section on beer, long a staple of both counterculture and faire: "The Renaissance faire entered the history of beer in the United States as an early location where dark beer, ale, and mead were sold, and for almost all visitors, tasted for the first time [...] To do this necessitated having the beer shipped directly from Sussex, England, to the faire, a fact that is singled out by much local newspaper coverage during the 1960s." It's hard to imagine how strange and strong English real ale might have been to the American palate used to weak lagers like Budweiser and Coors, typically the only thing easily found in the dark ages of American brewing, which ended in the 1980s with the explosion of craft beer and microbreweries. For this alone I deem the faire an important cultural force. In spite of this, beers on tap at this particular faire were more or less what you might get at a decent sports bar: Bass, Blue Moon, Miller Genuine Draft, Widmer Hefeweizen, Guinness, Dos Equis, etc.: I saw no sign of cask-conditioned ale or any of the hundreds of interesting microbrews now widely available.

4 — In spite of its recent craft renaissance, I would strongly suggest you avoid the mead. Some things should remain artifacts of the past.

display just below the fur-lined handcuffs, and so on). There are a lot of swords; a few improbable chain mail bikinis you might remember from viewings of schlock eighties films like *Red Sonja* or the covers of fantasy novels; places with names like the Horn Shoppe (which sells horns for "Drinking, Blowing and Combination"); scads of fat kids; scantily clad teens; a large proportion of people dressed like pirates; jousting; funnel cakes; some kind of doubtfully medieval-themed nachos; a couple dressed up as garden gnomes; falconry; rides; games; tests of skill; cleavage displayed by anyone with half a boob to boost up and display; heraldry; courtliness; staves; knaves; sad imprisoned hawks and owls; and ATM after ATM to facilitate your hunger for more of it, whatever "it" is that you're looking for more of here. Though an amusing sign, conscious of its anachronism, claims, "We accept Lady Visa and Master of the Card," cash is preferred.

In America — and certainly in Phoenix — we do love a spectacle, not to mention a Frozen Princess Latte. Clearly many of us are here just for the spectacle. All these playtrons, all these people: if this many people come out to see something, then we should come see it, too. But the real appeal of the faire appears to be the opportunity it affords for role-playing. For an afternoon you may choose to discard your regular life, put on the garb, and party like it's 1399. Sure, it's stratified: know your place, vassal! Of course, though we prefer to think otherwise, our ordinary lives are severely stratified, too; how recently have you dined with royalty (or with a Hollywood star, or a Pulitzer Prize winner, or the president)? Here you can, kind of, at the Pleasure Feast, twice daily, at noon and 2:30 p.m., for $69.95 if you purchase tickets in advance.

A lot of Americans, obviously, like to role-play, and not just in the bedroom: if you count computer and video games and tabletop RPGs, or if you look at what you do on your smartphone when in the post office line or driving, there are a whole lot of us who enjoy disappearing into a character. Reading fiction is a kind of role-playing, too. Sure, we can't always control the characters (let alone the plot), but the best novels involve us via a deep and prolonged identification that's very much like playing a role. And how else do sports work, if not via a kind of imaginative identity transfer? It's not as if rooting for the Green Knight in a joust is much different than cheering for the Crimson Tide as they uproot and steamroll Notre Dame. In all these pursuits we lose ourselves, if we're lucky, for a moment, and in the clash we feel alive by proxy.

It's hot. We enter through the gate. I feel alive just inside the door when we see a giant treant (a huge, living, speaking tree; I'm using the *D&D* term — Tolkien calls them ents) stretch out its huge tree branch arms to encircle a teen. A sign tells us he is called the Greenman. We have stepped out of the real world.

In addition to the role-playing inherent to dressing in garb or throwing out a few thees, thous, and huzzahs, there are also plenty of actual games to play inside. On the car ride up, I've been talking about the ax-throwing from two years ago that I remember I was totally great at, though we don't see that yet. First there's the Dragon Climbing Wall, the High Stryker (one of those ring-a-bell-with-a-hammer deals), the-darts that you throw at balloons to win prizes. None of this is very interesting, we think, and it's hardly Middle Age–appropriate (you see how it is easy to slide into authenticity-nitpicking, itself a kind of sport). There's a "medieval" version of the bar game shufflepuck (which I love), in which you slide a "medieval" beer stein down a sawdust-coated wooden lane and try to land it on a bull's-eye. It is called "New World Slider Joust." It is real hard. Why do people even enjoy playing these games, I wonder? The odds are against you. You know this. But then there's Vegas, the lottery, carnival games. Thank god the dream — the hope — is more powerful than the math.

Jon's face lights up as we approach the archery range, which has no prizes, but you do get to rent arrows and shoot them into a giant purple octopus and a very large evil prince figure pinned to a backdrop of hay bales. This is surprisingly enjoyable. It is evident that Jon has discovered a hidden talent that will be useful in the end days. Actually quite a few skills demonstrated at the faire — blacksmithing, glassblowing, ax-throwing, hypnotism, falconry, even henna tattooing and belly dance — may prove useful when the apocalypse arrives.

Jon and I agree that the "& Artisan Marketplace" part is more apparent on this visit than last time, or perhaps we're just noticing it more because of Rubin's book (and herein is much of the pleasure and usefulness of *Well Met*). Perhaps the recent resurgence of the handmade and DIY in the age of mechanical reproduction and digital commerce (Etsy, etc.) is partly responsible for this, but it's been a part of Renaissance faire culture from the beginning. "The English country fairs on which the first Renaissance Pleasure Faire was modeled occurred at the marketplace; practically speaking, they were seasonal celebrations organized around commerce," Rubin writes:

> From the beginning, the faire's organizers imagined selling not only food and drink [...] but also handmade crafts. And although the faire's origins may have been in performance, this craft vending quickly turned out to be not only one of the most popular aspects of the faire but also one of the most influential and central to its self-conceptualization.

In fact, performance and craft are not so far apart. For those of us who grew up without instruction in the physical, here you can actually learn how to make a thing, preferably with a plastic cup of mead on hand and ready for the quaffing. You can buy things from humans crafted by human hands. Even if our parents never taught us the domestic arts and we grew up educating ourselves on the best way to microwave pot pies (bad idea: you want to pop that shit in the oven to brown the crust properly, even if takes an hour), we still respect people who can make things — who have made things. There is an obvious power in it. They carry themselves with the swagger of the accomplished.

Despite its origins in hippie resistance to commercialism, then, there's no denying that the contemporary faire, what with the Monk's Bakery and Cappuccino Inn, and the ubiquitous signs directing you to ATMs, is a commercial space, and that this fact helps account for Ren faires' continued existence. (There's only so much money to be made, one imagines, in blacksmithing demonstrations.) While Rubin demonstrates that the faire's antiestablishment tendencies still exist, she also finds that they have had the edges sanded down somewhat over five decades. The term widely used by Rubin's interviewees (and Rubin herself) for this slow middling and settling is *Disneyfication*, which began, unsurprisingly, in the 1980s. Rubin writes that this process is widely lamented by faire workers, who, though they understand the commercial pressures of events of this size,

> still feel that an excessive level of rationalization and a policy of playing it safe so as not to alienate the "lowest possible denominator" (as one dedicated visitor puts it) has had a high cost in terms of creative values and spontaneity and has turned some faires into "shopping malls with entertainment," a phrase that came up often enough to cause one to wonder how commonly, and through what media, it is circulating. [A performer] reminded me that a more anarchic, less regimented philosophy is what allowed the faire to develop into the financial success that brought mandates of increased regimentation to it.

Rubin's interviews with faire veterans remind me of the laments of those self-proclaimed weirdos and outsiders involved in the early days of Silicon Valley (another California phenomenon, we duly note) who have since been corporatized and 401(k)-ed and groomed. Innovation often arises from play, from unorganized and chaotic forces, but long-term success breeds (and requires) some degree of organization and rationalization. Still, Rubin reminds me in our conversation that the faires are yet quite various. Some, like Arizona's, are highly corporatized, while others, "run by individuals rather than corporations with New York boards of directors," try harder to hold the line against anachronism and consumer creep. Faires in Maryland and Oregon, for instance, remain more historical, artisanal, and idiosyncratic than the Arizona faire. In fact, Rubin notes that faires are largely tech-free spaces, aside from patrons' inevitable cellphones:

> For the most part, there's no amplification, no machines. At the very beginning of the faire, there was this whole idea of the 60s generation saying no to the machine, as the Berkeley Free Speech movement said, and now we have this time where the machine is something totally different [...] [T]here are ways in which Internet culture allows people for whom the faire is very important to prolong it in the off-season as they're in touch with each other in all these different ways. But then, when they go to the faire, they put it all away, and they're very attracted to that.

FAIRES STILL HAVE THE REPUTATION — well-deserved, as Rubin points out — for sexual permissiveness, and that's part of the draw. This being America, that the presence of sex makes the faire appealing to some also makes it appalling to others. It's not as central in this faire as I expected, but it's certainly here, as I discover when I head into the Metal Shoppe to look at the chain mail bikinis, which are gratifyingly real, if of dubious utility. In a caption of women in chain mail outfits, Rubin writes, wryly: "Women at the faire frequently reframe the martial implications of chain mail." I consider buying one as a joke for my wife — or for myself — but worry about the marital implications. When I come out of the Metal Shoppe, Clint has taken up residence on a wooden bench. I join him there to watch the sword swallower. (His name is "Thom Sellectomy"; the tagline on the sign that abuts the stage reads: "He can't help the way he is!") Long wands of metal disappear, one after another, into his mouth. Jon can't handle this particular brand of entertainment, it appears, so he's wandered off into the shade. Clint and I gape, impressed. It's hard not to appreciate this skill, which does seem almost like a form of magic.

We finally happen upon the ax-throwing, and of course Clint goes over immediately and starts dropping dollars on the bar. The skinny hawker kid hands us three axes for $3, which we're meant to throw into another stack of hay bales 20 feet away like the fine examples of ax-hurling masculinity we surely are. There's a little painted heart that if you hit you get a crappy prize. Kid has some advice for us on how to throw these axes — the secret is ... Whatever, sirrah, I say, I'm Nordic. This is my ancestral skill, handed down by my forefathers through the mists of time. I line up and launch, and ... my first ax clatters weakly to the floor. I look at Clint, and he buries one in the target, biceps flexing, like a golden, glowing god. His face swells with virility; my face just swells. I look back and Jon is helpfully shooting video. Two axes later I do finally hit the target ... with the handle. A child gives me the thumbs-up, and I turn away, again unmanned.

I tell myself that perhaps, along with halitosis and an instinct for parallel parking, my ancestors bequeathed me a skill that I will yet discover, but not this day. Clint has stuck all three axes in a nice pattern around the heart, like he's ready to cut it out and consume it to level up and double in strength and size. He receives his prize, which is a paper certificate. What does it say? I can only guess: this knowledge is for the victor.

Exhausted from demonstrating my inadequacy, I grab another ale and immediately feel better. "Huzzah for the good tipper!" the vendor calls out as I disappear a buck into the elaborate wooden tip jar. Perhaps *this* is my skill.

Aside from the thumbs-up kid, my companions, and Christophe the Insulter, whom everyone avoids but watches from afar, no one's here to mock me, not really. There is, however, a long tradition of faire attendees being mocked. If we're looking to understand the historical or contemporary cultural significance of the faire, Rubin suggests, we must pay attention to "the terms on which it is commonly derided." So, in my favorite chapter, she interviews some haters — both in person and online, where, as we all know, the haters are particularly strong. "Probing the reasons for [their hate]," she finds, "yields some useful insights about the way both the faire and ridiculing the faire function in tandem as collective social practice." According to Rubin, "contempt for the faire falls almost exclusively into three major categories ... nonconformity, clothing, and body size. "In particular, she discovers, "[t]he wearing of tights by men comes up in the majority of mocking accounts of the faire, the practice seemingly inspiring an outpouring of dread about what constitutes proper masculinity":

> The sheer frequency with which the specter of "men in tights" is invoked reveals that tights are operating as a sort of code or shorthand for transgressive male behavior, not unlike the wearing of long hair did in the 1960s and 1970s [...] To put it more simply, anxious discussions of male tights-wearing vis-à-vis the faire are frequently tied to what we now call homophobia [...] If "men in tights" operates as a kind of shorthand for gender disobedience in men, women at the Renaissance faire are most widely punished for departures from mainstream beauty culture in terms of body size.

While Rubin's analysis of the gender politics of the faire is broadly convincing, it is odd that, in order to be able to commit acts of contemporary gender disobedience, playtrons choose to dress and conduct themselves according to a vague reading of a repressive feudal code with deeply rigid gender roles. As Rubin reminded me during our interview, "that's the oxymoron of any kind of historical recreation": donning the clothes of a medieval character doesn't necessarily mean subscribing to the whole medieval mindset, but it does mean layering past on present and perhaps escaping from both. What we're experiencing here is the past, but slant, filtered through what we Americans imagine, dream, or want the Renaissance to have been like.

When we speak on Skype, after I've returned from the Arizona festival, I ask Rubin about her focus on gender and sexuality at the expense of class or race, which receive only a few pages each in *Well Met*,[1] and she says that it was the most obvious lens she found, perhaps because of the performativity of the faire (and gender), and since the faire's critics mostly object to it on the grounds of gender and sexual norms. But these questions remain intertwined with class:

> We wear clothes to show people — clothes have always been connected to class. That's one thing they're *for*. Here men prefer the garb of the upper class. They want as much velvet and lace as they can put on themselves. Some of them are very clear that this is not something they get a chance to do outside the faire. Women tend to go for dressing like what inside the faire is called a wench. They want to be able to be sexually aggressive. So they tend to wear lower-class clothing and call out semi-obscene things.

Rubin was surprised to find that attendees of the contemporary faire, despite its early links to the student radical movement, are largely working class: "To learn that the faires switched to being a working class thing largely: I didn't see that coming." Reinforcing her argument about the faire as a space to perform otherness, she writes that

> the largest subgroup of playtrons — in Massachusetts, Maryland, Texas, California, Georgia, and Wisconsin — identifies as blue collar. Given time to compose their answers (as opposed to answering on the fly in the midst of faire activities), this identification was often articulated in ways that expressed a tension between faire identity and mundane identity.

It is easy to mock the faire for its seeming weirdness and its lack of historical depth or fidelity. But that's partly what's so amazing about it: of course it's easy to mock. It offers itself openly to haters, and, in so doing, transcends their hatred. Any group

---

1 — Though, in our conversation, she directed me to one of the more spectacular moments that occurred in her research: "Some people made these beautiful gestures that just spoke for themselves. One of them was in Maryland: a playtron, an African-American man at the faire wearing nothing but tattered pants and chains. That said more than my whole book."

engaged in collective play — going for it this deeply, this often, on this scale — requires you to buy into its magic or risk being a chump. That's a good definition of counterculture right there: a collective opt-in hallucination, an afternoon of play, an experience that's preferable, at least for a day, to your job at the private prison in Florence, Arizona. At the faire, you have two choices: either opt in or float above it, aloof, bored, cargo-shorted, incapable of feeling wonder or losing and thereby finding yourself. Will you like what you find?

feeling ill, his intestinal distress providing a touch of conspicuous medieval authenticity. A hero feeling sick is a sad thing, so we decide to head quickly toward the exit. A court processes by us: we saw them earlier, at "The Princess Meets the Suitors, Scene 1." The last woman to pass has her breasts bustiered to the level of her face.

Jon's getting greener as we evade the Greenman's bark arms yet again and pass through the gate and back into the reality of outer Phoenix, flat and dusty, unmagical, hot as ever, still very much ourselves. We talk again of dressing up next year. We're thinking monks. Or maybe grim reapers, in robes. We can just silently point at people until they freak. We should go earlier, before it gets this hot. I threaten to come in drag, thinking back to the possibilities offered by a chain mail bikini. We find our car safe in the Knave lot, and roll the windows down as we hit the road, going east then south, back through an infinity of cactus. We know we'll miss "Knighting Ceremony," "The Suitors Compete, Scene 2," and "Royal Dating Game & Finale." But I think we all know it has a happy ending. ✦

Two Questions for Rudolfo Anaya

DANIEL OLIVAS

Rudolfo Anaya's 1972 novel Bless Me, Ultima *is one of the foundational texts of Chicano literature. Born to a family of ranch hands and farmers, Anaya grew up in rural New Mexico before moving to Albuquerque as an adolescent. Anaya spent two years trying to find a mainstream publisher for the book before going with Berkeley's Quinto Sol, a publishing house dedicated to the Chicano Movement. The book was an immediate success and continues to be widely read and assigned in college classes.*

Daniel Olivas interviewed Anaya about his latest novel, The Old Man's Love Story. *It is a book of mourning, based in part on the death of Anaya's wife of 44 years: "An anguish deep in his soul sprouted and set loose suffocating tentacles. He had not cried since childhood, but now he cried. The loss he felt wracked his days and nights. He had entered a time of grieving, not knowing if it had an end."*

But it is also a realistic reflection on aging. Anaya writes about surviving on social security, dealing with ageism, the way an old man can be hard on himself: "You had your chance, chango. Is that what you had become? A monkey man? Walking around like a chimp on his knuckles. Dragging his lame leg..." Anaya's protagonist complains about the decay of his body with honesty, tinged with both humor and fear: "Old people know bathrooms are dangerous places."

The Old Man's Love Story *is an intense philosophical meditation on death, memory, and meaning, or as Anaya puts it, "Love, grief and memory. The sad, symbolic world of three, the old man's trinity." In the midst of the suffering and self-abasement are moments of redemptive poetry. "Life ends," he writes, "like shining from shook foil."*

DANIEL OLIVAS:
The Old Man's Love Story grows out of your experiences with the 2010 passing of your beloved wife, Patricia. It almost feels like a personal journal (though in the third person). Did the manuscript grow out of journal writing? Why did you decide to call it fiction rather than a memoir?

RUDOLFO ANAYA:
The publisher called it a novella, some book reviewers have called it a memoir — I guess it's a mixed genre. Let's call it a story that grew out of personal experiences that I then wrote from a prose/fiction perspective, that is, my perspective as storyteller. It could not be otherwise. I only have myself to tell the story.

My strong suit is writing fiction. My search for the true nature of reality has led me to believe that memoirs are really fictions. We cannot capture the true experience we write as memoir. As we write what we "really believed happened" we create a story around the experience, and since that past experience now lives in memory, we compose a story (fiction) as we write the memory. All we write is fiction, and that's the beauty of writing memories to share with others. It's by using the elements of fiction, basic storytelling, that stories come alive. The imagination thrives by using the elements of storytelling.

And no, I didn't keep a journal. The chapters I wrote are themselves the journal of my journey through grief, love, and memory. The journey continues. I am still writing the story every day. If I write the passages in my mind, the old man's story would grow and grow. The book by now would be 20 or 30 times bigger.

Daniel Olivas:
In the preface, you state, in part: "The old man's wife dies, but her spirit is still with him, and her essence lives in him. But if the life they once shared lives on only in fading memories, what happens if those memories die?" In your case, this really isn't an issue because many of those memories are now in this novella that readers can experience (in a sense) for generations to come. In other words, one can argue that your love of and life with Patricia have now been immortalized. Is that one reason you decided to write this book?

Rudolfo Anaya:
Yes, some of the memories my wife and I shared are written into *The Old Man's Love Story*, but a million other memories are not recorded, and they will never be recorded. This is a truth the old man learns, and so do I as I tell the story. Of all the memories ever held by us humans on earth, only an infinitesimal amount survive. The great maw of time swallows everything, and time is a simple concept, or a way of saying, we forget. We forget everything.

Writing was a way to spill out the emotions I was experiencing. I did think along the way I was writing to others who had gone through loss of a loved one. I did not think of immortalizing the love my wife and I shared, or at least not until the final chapter. Death comes to us all; the old man has accepted this natural consequence. Is there an afterlife? As a shaman, the old man has caught glimpses of a truer essence beyond the veil that separates different realities. What he believes of the afterlife is an important theme in the book. In the end he believes he will be with his wife, but I don't sketch out the geography of his belief. Let the reader believe what he or she will believe. But do believe in love.

Coloring Outside the Lines

MARIA BUSTILLOS

Racecraft: The Soul Of Inequality in American Life is the first book I've read on the subject of race that speaks accurately to my lived experience. The average writer on race, whether his subject is sociology, politics, or cooking, is liable to draw a line around one kind of people, and base all his reasoning on matters relating to what is inside versus what is outside of that line. By contrast, the authors of *Racecraft*, Karen E. Fields and Barbara J. Fields (who are academics, and sisters — Barbara a historian, and Karen a sociologist) have undertaken a great untangling of how the chimerical concepts of race are pervasively and continuously reinvented and reemployed in this country, all without drawing a single circle themselves. Instead, they describe the circles drawn by others, you might say, and patiently erase each one. "Racism is first and foremost a social practice [...] an action and a rationale for action," the Fieldses write. Though the concept of race has no genetic or scientific basis, the hierarchical structures we've built using this false idea are alive and well, and we're all complicit in their persistence.

The flavor of the Fieldses' reasoning is evident from the first sentence of the authors' note that precedes the text:

> Some readers may be puzzled to see the expression *Afro-American* used frequently in these pages, *African-American* being more common these days. We do not take a dogmatic view on such terminological questions, preferring the approach of our grandmother, who used all but two of the terms that prevailed in her day (she died in 1987, just short of ninety-nine): Colored, Negro, Afro-American, and black. She used the term *nigger* and its close South Carolina cognate *nigra* only when quoting

> others with disapproval. Although we leave our fellow citizens to their own choice, we prefer *Afro-American*. We prefer it because it is time-honored, having deep roots in the literary life of American English. Moreover, it leaves room for useful distinctions. Karen's husband Moussa Bagate, a naturalized American citizen born in Ivory Coast, is an African-American. Barack Obama, the child of a Kenyan father and a Euro-American mother, is an African-American. Karen and I, like Michelle Obama, are Afro-Americans. Karen's daughter Maïmouna, the child of an African-American like the Obamas' daughters, and an Afro-American, may choose whichever term she likes.

Lucidity, insight, elegance, inclusiveness, friendliness, a keen sense of history: it's all there, and sets the tone for the rest of the book. This passage made me think, too, of my own approach to "terminological questions." I'm the first one in my family born in this country; my parents came to Long Beach, California — my father from Caracas, and my mother and her family from Havana — in 1958. I spoke Spanish before I spoke English. Today when people ask me whether I speak Spanish fluently I might say yes, or if my interlocutor really knows Spanish well I tell the truth, which is yes, with the vocabulary of a somewhat foul-mouthed eight-year-old. My cousin Zulema, who arrived here as a teenager, has a slight Cuban accent still; her sister Teresa, who was four or five, has no accent at all. Teresa speaks Spanish at work — she's a publishing executive, plus which she is a brain — so her Spanish accent is superb, and she writes far better than any of the rest of us do. When I try to have a real conversation in Spanish, I spend half the time asking, *Cómo se dice* "bicameral legislature"? *Cómo se dice* "food processor"? Etc.

All this by way of saying that my Americanness marked me in my family as much or more than my Latinness did in school. Nobody from an immigrant background ever quite fits in. This is a significant thing I have in common with my husband, an Englishman born in Malawi and educated in England; a lack of deep roots in the place and culture where you were born creates a distinct kinship between people, no matter where they're from. What it really means is that you grow up something of a chameleon.

I was very young when I understood that sometimes a person's mind could change about me completely, right before my eyes. I'd be the same on the inside, but found that I might really shock someone by speaking Spanish (it might be a comforting kind of shock, or a disquieting one); or by speaking English (ditto). That is to say, there's nothing unusual about surprising people, but what I'm talking about is a more elemental shift: I thought you were *this kind of person*, and now I realize you're *this kind.* And even as a child I would fleetingly reflect: Well, you thought wrong. You know no more about me than you did before; I am just myself, a person.

How best can I connect with you? Will you prefer me to be a Cuban woman, I have the tools for that. Or I can seem basically "white" too, if that's easier for you. My skin is just pale or olive enough that my background isn't easy to determine; when I'm in Europe people ask me whether I'm Greek or Italian. When in Los Angeles, where I live, people ask me if I am Mexican. All that is very natural and has never concerned me in the least. Indeed, it's a weird advantage that I have only recently come to appreciate fully. In a certain way, blue-eyed blondes are in the same condition as African Americans in most parts of America: they carry on their skin information that telegraphs a set response from a lot of people. But with me, you can't exactly be sure "what I am" until I've had a chance to take your measure. If you have preconceptions you'll slip up, almost certainly reveal more than you intended, give me a chance to recalibrate. So that we can talk.

Maybe because it's in my nature to want to communicate with people, pretty much at all costs, I never felt the need or desire to identify particularly with in-groups of any kind. I would no more give up my Latinness for an absolute assimilation into white culture than I would give up *Star Wars* for Dostoevsky, or my native Valley Girl-ish Long Beach accent for an *NPR*-correspondent one. In my ideal universe, I'd be able to speak every language fluently, understand all cultures everywhere.

But obviously I can't, and *Racecraft* helps explain why not. There are a lot of things that divide Americans from one another: class, ethnicity, sexuality, gender, language. Race provides some of the thickest, most stubborn walls between us, and despite being discredited as a scientific concept, it is still a sure-fire conversation-stopper. In asserting that race does not exist, the Fieldses do not argue, as many have since the election of Barack Obama in 2008, that we are now living in a "post-racial society." (Indeed, the Fieldses cite Obama not as a symbol of the end of racism but as a kind of living avatar of racecraft: "Even as commentators at the time of Obama's election claimed to discern the coming of a 'post-racial' era, their very harping on Obama as a 'black president' reprised an age-old feature of racecraft: the turning of one person of African descent into a synecdoche for all.") "Whatever the 'post' may mean in 'post-racial,'" the Fieldses write, "it cannot mean that racism belongs to the past":

> Something is afoot that is the business of every citizen who thought that the racist concepts of a century ago were gone — and good riddance! — as a result of the Civil Rights Movement. The continued vitality of those concepts stands as a reminder that, however important a historical watershed the election of an African-American president may be, America's post-racial era has not been born. Perhaps it can be made if America lets those concepts go. But if they are hard to let go, why is that? What are they made of? How do they work?

That's what *Racecraft* provides: a working model of how "race" operates in American society. In their introduction, the Fieldses distinguish between "three different things: race, racism, and racecraft":

> The term *race* stands for the conception of the doctrine that nature produced humankind in distinct groups, each defined by inborn traits that its members share and that differentiate them from the members of other distinct groups of the same kind but of unequal rank. [...] Fitting actual humans to any such grid inevitably calls forth the busy repertoire of strange maneuvering that is part of what we call *racecraft*. [...] *Racism* refers to the theory and practice of applying a social, civic, or legal double standard based on ancestry, and to the ideology surrounding such a double standard.

In other words: if there's no rational basis for racial discrimination, where does it even come from? It works like this: *racecraft*, a kind of magical thinking that is ready, even eager, to embrace insane notions from eugenics to the Bell Curve, is everywhere employed to lend credibility to the illusion of something called *race*. Racecraft fixes the illusion of race in the cultural consciousness as a reality, thereby creating a basis for the many and various oppressions that constitute *racism*.

The Fieldses then go on to break down how the magical concept of race implicitly provides political and philosophical cover for class oppression, "the need to manage politically the radical redistribution of income toward the well-to-do and the suffocation of public sentiment favorable to civil rights." The long history of racecraft has produced a whole a host of confused ideas, experiences, and values, all based in a false inequality that has by now become utterly entrenched and institutionalized.

Racecraft methodically constructs an argument that should be self-evident, but isn't: equality isn't a matter of noble idealism, but a plain truth. It's not a utopian dream to be aspired to, but reality always, and reality now. Human beings are already factually equal in everything that matters, down to the molecules of our DNA (which, they remind us, cannot be analyzed to determine the color of a person's skin). And yet discourse after discourse finds a way to rank us, divide us, and create measurements of status linked to race. What use are these artificial layers of status and privilege, when there are seven billion of us in the exact same condition? Scared, fragile, and — above all — temporary?

In my lifetime, "racism" has generally been taken to mean a form of oppression inflicted by white people of privilege upon the rest of us. But in the Fieldses' view, racism is a form of oppression created by the illusion of "race," which is in turn created everywhere, by everyone, through the weird occult science of racecraft (which, as they point out, is every bit as mythical, and powerful, as "witchcraft" was in the Middle Ages). Racecraft is practiced all around us, and by all of us, by those who view themselves as the victims and opponents of racism as surely as by those who are most obviously guilty of it. "Distinct from *race* and *racism*," they write, "*racecraft* does not refer to groups or to ideas about groups' traits [...] It refers instead to mental terrain and to pervasive belief [...] Do not look for racecraft, therefore, only where it might be said to 'belong.'"

One can be a non- and even antiracist, in other words, and still practice racecraft. "Racecraft operates on both sides of the screen," the Fieldses insist:

> It provides a template for understanding inequality whose taken-for-granted rules are so pervasive that knock-off versions of them move through the echelons. At a high school in a neighborhood where young black men had attacked Mexican immigrants, black students disparaged black classmates from backgrounds poorer than their own. In the same neighborhood, Mexican-Americans who had been born in the United States disparaged classmates born in Mexico. A black sophomore at a high school in the neighborhood apparently felt no stirring of either irony or historical memory when he pulled out of moth balls an old standard of segregationists: "I've got nothing against [Mexicans]. They work for my Moms. One even made me breakfast this morning."

Anybody can point in any direction and see inequality being constructed in real time, in exactly the manner the Fieldses describe above. Here, too, is a useful way to interpret conservative accusations of "reverse racism," so long bandied about by the likes of Rush Limbaugh. There are conservatives who would nominally agree with the Fieldses that race doesn't exist, an attitude exemplified by satirist Stephen Colbert's oft-repeated dictum "I don't see race." Bragging that you are "race-blind" to score political points is intrinsically nonsensical, something like saying you are "aura-blind" or "mark-of-the-beast-blind." But the corollaries that conservatives draw from this idea, by seeking to ignore or deny the long history of racial oppression in America (say, by opposing the Voting Rights Act or affirmative action) are certain to intensify rather than alleviate inequality. If we are to transcend its evils, ignoring the historical practice and effects of racecraft is a wrong-way strategy.

And we are indeed largely going about our altering our "race consciousness" in a counterproductive way. Reading *Racecraft*, I was irresistibly reminded of the story of The Entryway, a 2010 blog written by the white Los Angeles journalist Devin Browne. In January of that year, Browne arranged to move in with an undocumented Mexican family in MacArthur Park, along with photographer Kara Mears (also white). The fact of the reporters' whiteness was interestingly jarring in itself, drawing attention to the fact that hardly any white people ventured into MacArthur Park, ever — the first question raised by the Entryway project being, why not?

Browne's posts were extraordinarily personal and immediate, as were Mears's beautiful, intimate photographs. This blog embraced culture shock, rather than shying away from it. An early entry examined the fact that Browne's new housemates, Juan and Maria, had no particular interest in learning English (they weren't planning on staying in the United States permanently). Browne compared their lack of interest in English to her own father's attempts to learn Spanish, and to her parents' efforts to "expose their children to other cultures" in the bourgeois American manner. Another post recounted a night when the police mistook Browne's house for a neighboring one that had allegedly been harboring gang members. Here she explored the difference between her attitude toward the police and that of her housemates.

Initially, there was a flutter of interest and buzz surrounding Browne and Mears's project. The following week, however, all hell broke loose. In a blog post titled "Safari in Los Angeles, in a home in MacArthur Park," reporter Daniel Hernandez pitched a fit over The Entryway, accusing Browne and Mears of "vanity," "self-satisfied gloating," and "voyeurism." "[I]f independent media workers (or wealthy foundations, or documentary filmmakers) truly care about giving voice to marginalized voices," he wrote, "they should empower immigrants and poor people to *tell their own stories*.

[…] MacArthur Park deserves better. 'The barrio will have its own voice,' another friend responds, a young immigration lawyer, and a native of the neighborhood. 'That's the only way it can be.'"

In short, there was a right way — indeed an "only way" — and a wrong way to report on MacArthur Park, and Browne and Mears were unfit even to try, according to Hernandez. His remarks set the tone for, and were cited by, a dozen or so similar posts that quickly appeared on websites like Racialicious, CyberFrequencies, and Guanabee, all of them full of accusations of "othering" and "patronizing" and "tourism," and attracting a hail of comments deploring "elitist sheltered hipster racists." None of these critics contacted Browne to ask for a comment. This, too, is how racecraft works: not only though the top-down perpetuation of an artificial hierarchical structure, but also through a corresponding denial of good-faith attempts to interrogate that structure from the outside. Any attempt at discussing someone else's "racial identity" — let alone making the suggestion that "racial identity" doesn't really exist — is itself almost certain to be attacked as racist.

At the time it seemed to me that all these commenters were missing the point. Browne appeared as a figure in her own story because the schism between herself and her subjects so clearly and honestly reflected the real schism in our city. Perhaps that's why former MacArthur Park resident Felipe Gonzalez wrote to congratulate her in a long letter that appeared in the 13th post at The Entryway, which included an interesting side observation:

> When I lived in that neighborhood, I never thought I would ever talk to a white person or trust a white person. My only recollections of white people in that neighborhood was the white cops that frisked you and mistreated you for no reason. If you were 10 years old or more and something went down in the neighborhood, they just stopped every boy and mistreated them.

This letter demonstrated that Gonzalez, at least, understood Browne's point perfectly, even if the self-appointed media guardians of MacArthur Park did not.

So here's what appears to have fueled the outrage from so many bloggers and commenters, long used to viewing the undifferentiated mass of "the voiceless" and "the disenfranchised" through a comfortable lens of liberal detachment that pleasantly blurs the relative disparity in education and ease enjoyed by the reporters who commonly write such stories. Having to face that disparity explicitly, in the inconveniently snow-white middle-class person of Devin Browne, created about a thousand kinds of useful discomfort. The reader was invited to consider his own relationship to our large and disadvantaged undocumented Latino population, and to the privileged, educated class that writes just enough about their condition to enable the rest of us to ignore it.

Another example of how racecraft works in practice is provided by "Mea Culpa," a piece by Phoenix Tso for the recently launched blog The Toast. In this piece, Tso described her anger at a white stranger who, in passing, said "ni hao" ("hello" in Chinese) to her as she read on a bench in the park. Tso is not Chinese; she was terrifically insulted by this remark, and instinctively replied, "Fuck you." "Ni hao," she claimed, was a casually racist remark, though no exact facts as to why she thought so are supplied in the piece (the rest of which details a few other, truly racist remarks made to her at other times, by other people). With respect to being addressed in Chinese, Tso writes, "Some of these attempts really are just someone's way of 'saying hello,' and some other times the intent is malicious."

> Either way, people don't realize how wearing it is to deal with someone who just seems interested in you because you're an Asian woman, who can't look past that fact. It's worse when it's a stranger, because you have no other information about them, and no chance to show them that you're more than just your gender or ethnicity. It's enough to make anyone defensive and suspicious, when these incidents add up over a lifetime.

Here's exactly what makes this an example not of racism, in the Fieldses' terms, but of racecraft: Tso was so conditioned by her anger about the legacy of "incidents [added] up over a lifetime" that she was, by her own admission, entirely robbed of her ability to see this other "ni hao"–saying person as a regular person, a fellow human being. Perhaps also to say to this other, ordinary, quite possibly well-intentioned person, "You nut, I am not Chinese." Or, alternatively, to ignore him, and just think, "Eh, whatever, I am busy reading."

So I had a decidedly negative reaction to this piece (very like that of Tso's friend Luke, whose Facebook comments on Tso's actions are quoted throughout). For Pete's sake, I thought exasperatedly, discern the man's intent before you go yelling "fuck you." My default position has long been that anyone with enough to eat and a clean, safe place to sleep is already privileged in all the ways that matter most. Each of us walks around with some kind of baggage, so we all have to let some things slide; to make too much of personal slights to oneself is a distraction and impairs your ability to put your shoulder to the wheel. Giving other people the power to disturb your equilibrium to such a degree is not empowerment, it is weakness: thralldom, even, to the good behavior of strangers, an uncertain quantity at best.

But the sad fact is that racecraft is the water we are all swimming in, and Tso's reaction was simply inescapable for her. People I don't know speak Spanish to me all the time, and also English, and other languages that I do not know, and always have; these experiences have shaped my own way of responding to such overtures as inevitably as Tso's experiences have shaped hers. (Which is to say, in my own case, pretty blandly, though as a younger woman I did resort to pretending not to understand unwelcome remarks in the street from time to time.)

Reading *Racecraft* helped to show me how Tso's baggage is no less ineluctable than anyone else's; it is all the result of an ongoing oppression with the authority of centuries behind it that we renew every day, all together. Though Tso's anger, the echo of a very old anger, also serves to perpetuate the oppression, my own impatience with her wasn't helping any, either. Nobody here is in the wrong, and yet somehow everyone is.

On the flip side, this analysis throws the klieg lights on our best weapon against racecraft: all our kindness and understanding for one another has a force behind it, too, the powerful result of the kindness and open-mindedness of centuries past. That is a shared mindset that also belongs to everyone, can be practiced by everyone, and conditions us to meet new people as equals while still making an accurate assessment of the costs of historical oppression. Everyone can take some advantage of the ability to be understanding and empathetic. Nobody can do it all the time! But, sometimes, we can.

Granted, this may be harder to do in times like ours, where people are unequal in an objective, economic sense. Beyond the anti-egalitarian suspicion harbored by writers like Hernandez and Tso toward people who attempt cross-racial communication lies a bigger, even more pervasive series of illusions: the individualist, hyper-competitive mindset of modern careerist/consumerist culture. This is a different kind of inequality from that underwritten solely by race, but is intimately related to it, involving concepts like "social mobility" and "elitism." Maybe the worst effect of racecraft, the key cog in the machinery of American inequality, is its implicit sponsorship of social Darwinism: it provides a quasi-rational undergirding to the purely social idea of a hierarchy, so that there is always one's "race" or "class" either to transcend, or to live up to. In this way, Americans are tacitly persuaded that they must compete with one another in order to climb some illusory ladder. We are not equal, not the same — that is the fraudulent premise granted at the outset: like it or not, there are always and will always be people "below" us, and people "above," and it's our job to "succeed" within that hierarchical framework. This means not only that others must be harmed so that one can rise oneself — we should feel mildly regretful but basically okay about that — but that the self and its "progress" is the center of life.

An institutionalized selfishness, in turn, opens the door for all the in-groups and isms, so that we can feel self-righteous about our narrow, solipsistic concerns: if the self is the center of your world, what the self identifies with and aspires to is king. It won't matter if we give up our basic decency, swear at a stranger in the park, or write pathetically rude, cruel comments on an internet message board, because our only real responsibility is to ourselves, and to the tribe(s) with which we selfishly and noisily identify. We don't have to try to understand anyone else, let alone our opponents. Why try to make common cause or even coexist with them? "Those people" don't count, and they hate us anyway!

In reading the Fieldses' book, I was recalled to so many scenes in my own life, such a jumbled mixture of impressions seen through this new and truer lens: times when my own children were embarrassed by my Latin background; showing a boyfriend how to salsa dance; friends laughing with delight at my mom's classic Ricky Ricardo Cuban accent, and teasing her by asking her to say in English, "Sure, I'll share a chair!"; traveling to Europe the summer after high school and, on a verdant hill near the Alhambra, hearing a group of handsome young people speaking Castilian Spanish for the first time; the sweet girls who've been cooking at Yuca's on Hollywood since back when it was still Casa Diaz. The way all these pieces of one life are caught up in sociopolitical hierarchies that, while one may not believe in them oneself, have implications that can't simply be wished away.

I can't remember a time I didn't understand very clearly that anyone who would try to offend you by saying some daft thing about your ancestry, your coloring, or the language you speak was an ignorant person, a basic saddo, someone to be pitied from as afar as possible. Lately, though, I no longer feel so separate from anyone. Detachment alone can't actively advance the cause of equality; it has to be tempered with the knowledge that we're all implicated in how we treat one another, and must therefore engage each person's convictions freely and in an open spirit, if we are ever to become a "post-racial" society. ✦

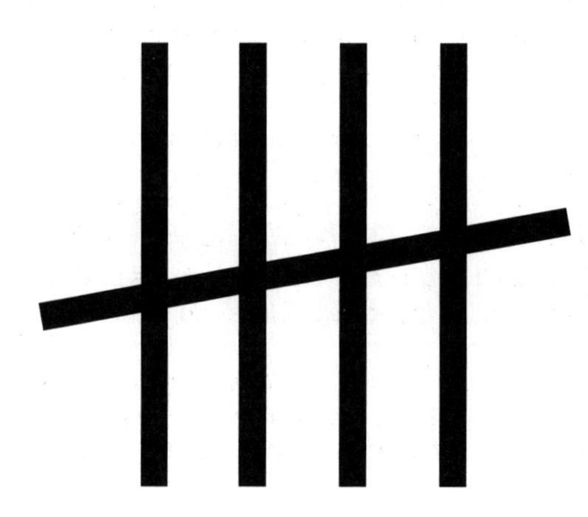

THE FIVE STAGES OF ART

TOM BISSELL

All forms of art proceed through five distinct stages.

The first stage hinges on the art form's ability to provide audiences with simple, childlike pleasure. The second stage begins when it attracts a formally inquisitive audience determined to figure out the art form, unlock it, somehow know it from the outside in. During the third stage, the art form appears interesting or worthwhile almost exclusively to those with a theoretical and/or practical interest - to the artists and their critics. By the time the fourth stage rolls around, the art form is "admired" by audiences while not actually having any audience to speak of. With the fifth stage, there are no artists left, only artisans.

I can think of no exceptions to this. Of course, forms of art that are essentially renewed by technology every few generations - music, for instance - can jump back and repeat stages, but forms of art that are largely indifferent to technological benefit cannot. The point is, all art forms eventually run out of audience. This is the way it is.

Painting and many of the visual arts are very nearly through to stage five. The novel has advanced alarmingly close to stage four. Filmmaking is well into, by my rough estimation, stage two.

It took me a while to realize we have nothing to fear from this.

Aliens

RACHEL KAADZI GHANSAH

"I cross out words so you will see them more: the fact that they are obscured makes you want to read them."

Jean-Michel Basquiat

"The letter is armed to stop all the phony formations, lies, and tricknowlegies placed upon its structure."

Ramm:ΣLL:ZΣΣ

"The ship I came here on vanished."

Palaceer Lazaro

For five hours, Rachel Jeantel, a childhood friend of Trayvon Martin, sat on the stand and tried to recount the last conversation they had before he was murdered. They had known each other since they were in elementary school. Rachel Jeantel was still a high school student when she not only tragically lost her friend but also became the lead witness for the defense in the highly publicized murder case that polarized America. It was a trial that would decide if George Zimmerman, the man who murdered Trayvon, would face justice. That she was just 19 years old, a teenager, shell-shocked and in mourning, were a few of the least-discussed qualities of Ms. Jeantel. Instead her size, her color, and her speech thrust her into the headlines. Jeantel is a heavyset young woman with brown skin. In the aftermath, even smart publications could not resist drawing comparisons between Ms. Jeantel and director Lee Daniels' unconfident, abused, broken bird Precious. It was a comparison that told us almost nothing about Rachel Jeantel and much more about people's expectations of women who look like Rachel Jeantel: primarily, that if you are heavy and have dark skin in America you shouldn't dare exist in real life. It was pretty inconvenient then, that on the stand, Ms. Jeantel — sotto voce too — refused to be anyone but herself. If Jeantel was anything for the two days she was on the stand, she was complex, a young woman who was gentle at times, insistent at others, the sort of girl who would roll her eyes one minute, and the next would end her answers with "sir"s. She was a young woman who freely admitted to struggling with literacy, but at the same time speaks three languages fluently.

"Are you claiming in any way that you don't understand English?" asked George Zimmerman's defense attorney, Don West.

"I don't understand you. I do understand English," said Jeantel.

"When someone speaks to you in English, do you believe you have any difficulty understanding it because it wasn't your first language?" asked West. Don West is the lawyer who took his own bleached-blonde daughters, Rachel and Molly, out to ice cream after he cross-examined Rachel Jeantel. Ice cream cones in hand, his daughters would later post on Instagram a picture of the moment with their dad, subtitled, "We beat stupidity celebration cones" with the hashtag "#dadkilledit."

"I understand English really well," said Jeantel.

When I watched Ms. Jeantel I did not get the sense that I was watching a young woman who did not understand English. I got the sense that Don West was not interested in understanding Rachel Jeantel. I got the sense that, to Mr. West, and much of the courtroom, Rachel Jeantel and Trayvon Martin might as well be aliens.

So Rachel Jeantel spoke the language she knew with conviction, because it is exhausting having to assert that your life has value, and there are times when English in its standard form cannot and does not express what it is like to have a friend shot for doing absolutely nothing wrong except being black and wearing a hoodie while going out for some candy.

This is to say, we battle for existence in real life as well on the page. We must defend our dreams and our daily lives. Rachel Jeantel's playfulness, her slang, her exasperation are now important parts of the record of the Martin trial, and expose not just who she was but who Trayvon Martin was as well. Whether she reads well or not, Rachel Jeantel authored for the court a narrative, scribbled in the margins, one of the few that will express how nonsensical the proceedings were for so many of us who watched. Words like Jeantel's — often expressed in far-out forms like graffiti and slang — trace the sense of feeling X-filed; they are the ways to acknowledge life in the bush of ghosts, and give names and sounds to the consciousness of radical world-building that the descendants of the African Diaspora have engaged in all around the world. This is the tradition Rachel Jeantel was practicing up on the stand: the art of being young, black, and incomprehensible.

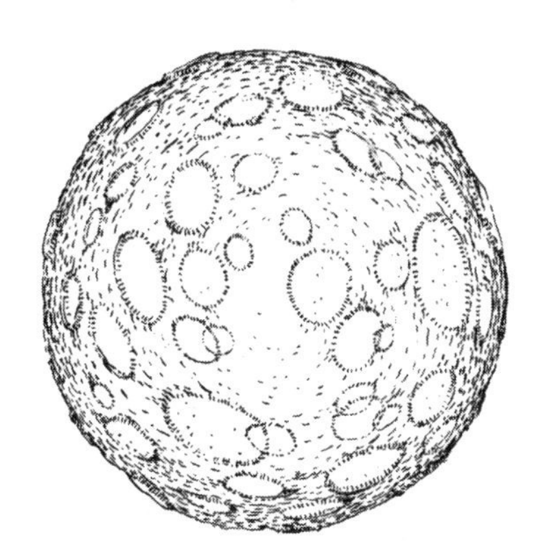

LIKE RACHEL JEANTEL, JEAN-MICHEL BASQUIAT was half-Haitian. But, besides bloodlines and shared languages, the most immediate, immutable connection that Basquiat shares with Jeantel might be that he also felt his own life called into question, as so many of us do when a fellow member of our community turns up dead, killed without due process. Michael Stewart was a young dreadlocked graffiti writer from Brooklyn who, while in the custody of 11 white members of the NYPD on September 15, 1983, mysteriously went unconscious and later died. And, just as Trayvon Martin, in the afterlife Stewart was denied justice by the courts. The police said it was a heart attack; his family's doctor said it was death by strangulation.

Stewart, a slight, easygoing Pratt student, was born and raised in Clinton Hill. On the night of his beating he was arrested and accused of defacing the First Avenue subway station. He fled, but was captured and taken to jail and then transported to Bellevue Hospital — at this point he was already unconscious. In the hospital after 13 days in a coma, he died without ever waking up. The senseless murder of a young black male artist from a middle-class home whose life in some ways so mirrored his own (Stewart at the time was dating Suzanne Mallouk, Jean's ex) would deeply fuck with Jean-Michel Basquiat. When he heard news of the murder, Basquiat began to draw black skulls. Later he would tell Suzanne, "It could have been me, it could have been me." The murder would inspire him to paint *Defacement* (*The Death of Michael Stewart*) (1983), in which two white policemen brandish billy clubs over a black figure who seems to have already become a ghost. Above the scene the word "DEFACIMENTO" is scrawled.

The murder of Michael Stewart disturbed Basquiat and his generation as much as the murder of Trayvon Martin has disturbed ours. Keith Haring would paint about it; Spike Lee's *Do The Right Thing* (1989) would draw cinematic attention to the chokehold and violence employed by the police in the neighborhoods they were supposed to protect. Like the murder of Emmett Till, these attacks remind us of things we would rather forget: that the more things change, the more they stay the same. So we need to know how to express the existential grief, the blood that falls on the leaves when it seems almost every generation of black people will be reminded at one point or another of the everlasting truth in Billie Holiday's "Strange Fruit."

We have to tell these stories in their own strange way. (DEFACEMENT? Meaning a wall, or Michael Stewart's face?) In her inability to form words, her occasional difficulty in articulating herself — something she explained multiple times was the result of grief and fear — Ms. Jeantel cracked open a conversation about how race and language work. In her insistence that she had to tell the story in her own way, from inside of a closet, full of silences and vagaries, and allegiances worth lying for, in her quiet sense of self-worth about herself and her dead friend and her occasional triumphant moments over the men who all but called her stupid, I don't think Rachel Jeantel is connected to Precious at all. I think she connected herself to the right to defiant invention that has long been a cornerstone of black language in the States.

America was not yet America when North Carolina in 1740 made it illegal to teach any enslaved person how to write. It would be the first step in a centuries-long campaign whose only aim was to prevent the instruction and education of black people in America. Now we forget how often and how strenuously we have been denied entrance into the bazaar of books, language, and letters. How often, like the Goths who sacked Rome, we've entered the written word as invaders, spray painters, and stealth soft speakers. In her essay "Positive Obsession" (1996), Octavia Butler writes about her trepidation, as a young black girl, upon entering a bookstore:

> I crept into my first bookstore full of vague fears. I had managed to save about five dollars, mostly in change. It was 1957 [...]
>
> "Can kids come in here?" I asked the woman at the cash register once I was inside.I meant could Black kids come in. My mother, born in rural Louisiana and raised amid strict racial segregation, had warned me that I might not be welcome everywhere, even in California.
>
> The cashier glanced at me. "Of course you can come in," she said. Then, as though it were an afterthought, she smiled. I relaxed.

> The first book I bought described the characteristics of different breeds of horses. The second described stars and planets, asteroids, moons and comets.

I like to imagine, from this moment, a young but already tall Octavia Butler leaving the restrictions of this earth to grow herself out of her lived condition in California and take her place among the stars as one of the greatest science fiction writers. But why do we still so often look to the unknown spaces, other languages, and new names? Why do we invent and stay rooted in a language that only we understand? I think black Americans have needed space and the realm of the incomprehensible — as a kind of haven, an alienated otherworld, whirling with unknowns and new freedoms for a very simple reason: because our real life here on earth has at times been more than a drag.

IN 1985, WILLIAM LABOV, a linguist at the University of Pennsylvania, would conclude at the end of a three-year National Science Foundation–funded study, that "there is evidence that, far from getting more similar, the black vernacular is going its own way." "The more we study and analyze," Dr. Labov said, "the more it shows the signs of people developing their own grammar." Despite the researchers' expectations that television and movies had exerted a "homogenizing" effect on American English, what they instead found was, because of "increasing racial segregation and isolation of urban blacks," the first and only contact many black people had with standard English and other dialects of English occurred when they entered schools. This is not to negate the fact that "millions of blacks speak standard English, and many more speak standard English, the black vernacular and white dialects, shifting from one to the other depending on the setting," according to the *New York Times* article that reported on the study. But as Labov explained, it illustrated a few things: that black vernacular was a "healthy, living form of language" with its "own grammar, which is very rich and complicated [...] developing its own way," and that "separate development is only made possible by separate living." It is this kind of linguistic divide that allowed the same person to be an easygoing, black boy to some and a potential criminal to others, a normal teen to his parents and a hoodie-wearing thug who deserved to die to Zimmerman's perverse supporters. These are acts of translation that could blinker anyone's sanity. It's like saying an apple is to a fruit as an orange is to a fruit. We are reminded that part of comprehending any language is understanding the trickery contained within it.

When, eight years later, the critic Mark Dery wrote "Black to the Future: Afro-Futurism

1.0" (1993), he posed a very serious question:

> Hack this: Why do so few African-Americans write science fiction, a genre whose close encounters with the Other — the stranger in a strange land — would seem uniquely suited to the concerns of African-American novelists? [...] They inhabit a sci-fi nightmare in which unseen but no less impassable force fields of intolerance frustrate their movements; official histories undo what has been done to them.

While Dery is correct to address this underrepresentation as a consequence of "separate living" and therefore raise the call for more Afro-futuristic writers of the conventional, pen and paper kind, it is worth noting that authorship and language for black Americans has always worked differently, and not just grammatically as Labov suggests. Rappers are writers. Graffiti artists are writers. There is an oral tradition in black culture that ignores the written word completely. The old question of what is an author has to be expanded itself to fit the wider loom of language that permeates black life. The danger is that "curated" conversations about what it means to be black now — to be stopped and frisked, targeted for arrest — are all too often held in spaces like universities, libraries, and museums that haven't quite figured out how to diversify or integrate their dialogues socioeconomically. All too often voices like Rachel Jeantel become foreign and are perceived to be the embarrassment.

In his book *Within the Context of No Context* (1981), George W.S. Trow writes of a young black man new to college, who felt the Dutch masters of the 17th century "belonged" to the white students in the room and he had no relation to them. After he said this to the class, many of the white students felt guilty and leapt to discuss their hegemony over the black student, but really, they were feeling for the first time ownership and euphoria. Trow wonders, "Had the young black man asked, 'Who is this man to you?' the pleasure they felt would have vanished in embarrassment." Today, too, there is a question about ownership, but the question is directed toward language. When Rachel Jeantel rolls her eyes, sucks her teeth, and gets visibly annoyed, she provokes us into wondering what form stories about the unthinkable should take, and what the language of trauma that stems from police brutality and violence should sound like. Who will own it?

In the Gagosian Gallery in downtown New York a few months ago, I stood behind three silver-haired white ladies with canes and watched them tremble before Jean-Michel's Basquiat's *Riding with Death* (1988). I had been living in the woods

of Louisiana and had timed my return to coincide, first, with the start of a friend's cancer treatment, and, second, with the last days of the gallery's Basquiat exhibit.

The ladies stayed as long as I did. There were about 20 of them all together; they were there as a senior group. And because of their walkers and canes they moved like a well-formed, hulking herd through the gallery. A mob of bebop baronesses, I thought.

In a small room we stared at *M* (1984, acrylic on wood), me and a few of them, in silence because it seemed to startle us all just how confidently, painted on a white picket fence, Death stared back.

A short one with a thin, drawn face and large, round eyes looked at the large image of a skeleton in blue, a death mask with a long, thick straight smile and yellow lips. Transfixed. She smacked her friend's elbow.

"Gladys, does your stomach have knots in it?" she asked.

"No," her friend said, furrowing her brow, "but my intellect does."

"What most people don't understand about Jean-Michel is that his crazy behavior had nothing to do with being an 'enfant terrible.'

Everything he did was an attack on racism and I loved him for this."
SUZANNE MALLOUK

FOR SOME STRANGE REASON there aren't many great books about Basquiat, or at least, books that are as brash and big as the artist himself. The catalog for his retrospective at the Whitney Museum in 1991 is seminal and excellent, but lately I have fallen under the hazy, lyrical love spell that Jennifer Clement captures in *Widow Basquiat* (2001).

Clement's biography of Basquiat's tempestuous relationship with Suzanne Mallouk is an unusual book because it is not about Basquiat, but rather about Mallouk, who was his girlfriend for many years. She was with him before the fame and the hard drugs, and when the drugs took his life in 1988 she was left behind. It is a slim book, elliptical at times, but what I like about it is how elegantly it gives flesh to Jean-Michel Basquiat's personality. In her small chapters, Clement avoids the academic discourse around Basquiat, and perhaps to some degree the art, to describe the interiors of Suzanne's observations and interactions with a brilliant young man, a cultural polymath with impeccable taste and a bad attitude, who so badly wanted not to give a fuck about the establishment and yet cared about it so deeply:

> One Thursday in 1982, Jean-Michel tells Suzanne to stand up and walk, they are going to the MoMA [...] At the museum Jean-Michel takes a bottle of water out of his coat and walks through the halls sprinkling the water here and there around him.
>
> "I'd piss like a dog if I could," he says, as they wander past paintings by Pollock, Picasso, Kline and Braque.
>
> Suzanne does not even ask what he is doing [...]
>
> "There are no black men in museums," he says. "Try counting..."
>
> Suzanne cannot find even one.

But like all of us, Basquiat struggled to detach his ego and identity from the establishment's caste system. Here is a story:

> Jean-Michel likes to take Suzanne to fancy restaurants. One night at one expensive Italian restaurant there is a long table with twenty white businessmen having dinner. Jean-Michel says, "They are the kind who have their own private jets."
>
> The businessmen stare, whisper racist remarks and drunkenly laugh at Jean-Michel. They think he is a pimp because he is black and has dreadlocks and is wearing messy clothes. They think that Suzanne is a prostitute. She is heavily made-up and has her hair teased up in a beehive.
>
> Jean Michel tells the maitre d' that he is going to pay for the businessmen's dinner. It costs him $3,000. This is how Jean-Michel laughs back.

In his essay for the Whitney's catalog, Robert Farris Thompson calls Basquiat's "self-creolization" a "major source of power." As an artist he implicitly understood that "the central problem of the West today" was the "urgent need of intelligences other than our own" and that in order to tell his story and share his "genius for social statement" he would need to know how to be "fluent in several languages and know how to fuse them to effect." In many ways, Basquiat's life and art testify to his generation's greatest gift: they taught the world how to mix, sample, spray, and cut from nothing, foreverness. For JMB, Clement writes, this meant telling his story in loud colors on a large scale versus the minimalist work of his peers, and to do this he needed to cut and compile his own vocabulary:

> He paints, pauses, picks up a book or magazine and when he finds a word or sentence that he likes he paints it on the board or canvas. There are codes: The crown is the logo from the t.v. show "The Little Rascals." He mixes Spanish and English [...] He paints kings wearing black crowns covered in tar and feathers [...] He writes "TAR" everywhere in thick dark strokes because, "I sometimes feel as black as tar."

In Clement and Mallouk's retelling of the Basquiat legend, JMB is no stolid folk hero. He is often smack-sick. He does horrible things to women. He is irreverent. He fills refrigerators with pastries when he is happy. He is generous and grand. He hands out $100 bills to bums. "He makes fun of everyone by wearing pseudo-African garb to important art openings. Jean-Michel paints *Obnoxious Liberals* because he says he is sick of liberal white art collectors." And often he is just plain magnificent, like when he says, "Boom for real!" when he finishes designing Billie Holiday's gravestone.

I like these edges. I like seeing how, while on his way to boldly go where no black man had gone before (especially in the art world), Basquiat was totally human. He was as fond of hip-hop and bebop as he was Maria Callas. He understood that by rearranging the codes, by toying with the expectations attached to blackness, the expectations of what he should be like as a black man in America — a king, or a piece property — he could *détourn* his "name" and identity and make his entire life into a performance of defiant, subversive strategy. I like the art in this kind of living, the kind they cannot teach you at any school: it must come from the *sangre*.

WHEN IT COMES TO EXPRESSING the surrealism of being young and urban in the 20th century, nobody did it more aggressively than the community of graffiti writers that painted in NYC's streets and subways in the seventies and eighties. While two writers, Julio 204 and Taki 183, are credited with starting the whole trend of tagging one's name on a subway train, by the time *The New York Times* profiled Taki in an article headlined "Taki 183 Spawns Pen Pals," he had found that lots of young people were willing to evade the police to communicate by scribbling. There are many brilliant writers that came out of this era: Keith Haring, Dondi White, Futura, SLAVE, Toxic, A-1. And while graffiti is an inherently defiant act of writing, often considered vandalism (especially after selling spray paints to minors was criminalized in 1972, forcing many young scribes to turn to theft to procure their writing utensils), it is not without its own rules and aesthetics. Reborn out of the burning Bronx and practiced monastically at night under the watch of the baseheads, graffiti defined the high art and the subculture of an entire decade.

Shortly after the graffiti artist (and sometime close friend of Basquiat) RAMM-:ΣLL:ZΣΣ died in 2010, the Suzanne Geiss Company Gallery put together a retrospective of his work. In the gallery, against the white walls, his art seemed to engage in combat against the space. In one room, a series of calligraphic alphabets, the building blocks of his theories, fought against their frames to be free. In another room, suspended from the ceiling were a fleet of "Letter Racers," made out of intricately glued-together pen caps, skateboards, and bits of found hardware. This airborne armada sloped down over a series of large paint-splattered and spray-painted canvases that hung on the walls, marking the perimeter, all of it glowing brightly, flashing an otherworldly message: that this was the 30-year life project of a man who, by piecing together broken pieces of his city that he found in the gutters, made a world of his own.

Decades before all of this, RAMM:ΣLL:ZΣΣ had been a kid from Queens who became a legend, if not a king, in the Bronx. The Bronx was where he spent his teen years becoming a pioneer in the world of graffiti, and a rapper of some acclaim. And he is forever frozen in hip-hop's first (and best) motion picture, *Wild Style* (1983). He appears at the end of the film, when, after the guy (Lee Quinones) gets the girl (Lady Pink) at the amphitheater in the park, he briefly raps onstage in a trench coat with a shotgun in an off-kilter, slant-rhymed way. He called the style, which would later influence the Beastie Boys and Cypress Hill, the Gangsta Duck. It was just one of the many characters who peopled his universe. In an interview clip, RAMM:ΣLL:ΖΣΣ can be seen trying his masks and bodysuits on. "You have a pimp," he says, pointing to a fedora-wearing creature with a fanged grill, "known as the Duck. This is the Gash/olear. This is the secretary," pointing to a mask with a hulking robotic face with a blond wig on. "This is the judge." A skeleton with a wizened face goes by the Reaper Grim. "There is a matron, and that is the bookie," he explains in a theatrical voice, the same kind a child will use to sound like a criminal: "He takes bets."

In 2006, the writer Greg Tate went to Tribeca, to the loft where RAMM:ΣLL:ΖΣΣ lived with his wife, to talk with the reclusive artist. Tate would describe him as being "still tall and rangy, though with the inevitable middleage spread that 44 years can put on a brother," and he would describe the apartment, known as the Battle Station, as being swollen with "sculptures (most prominently a four foot high gold painted replica of an Egyptian ankh symbol), costumes and toys." RAMM:ΣLL:ΖΣΣ would tell Tate there was more art, so much more; with no end in sight he had already taken over his mother's garage in Queens. I remember thinking at the time, *This man is inexhaustible* ... But he was not.

After RAMM:ΣLL:ΖΣΣ's death, *The New York Times* would try to situate his legacy. Was he "a hip-hop artist with visual-art leanings," "most important as a muse and scene maker," or "mainly a painter and sculptor whose frenetic genre-bending and wildly eccentric visual style obscured his seriousness"? Instead of answers, we are told that "RAMM:ΣLL:ΖΣΣ never made it easy to answer any of these questions." And yet one way to approach RAMM:ΣLL:ΖΣΣ is through the written word. That is what captivated him, not only as a graffiti writer but, later, as a theorist, as his attention turned from emblazoning his name on the "moving pages" of the city's subway trains to working with the alphabet as a living, active thing. He called his philosophy "Gothic Futurism," and he explained that "RAMM:ΣLL:ΖΣΣ" was not a name but rather an equation.

Words were the basis of his lifework, and he would confess to Dave Tompkins of *The Wire* that this work consumed him: "To wipe out a language and make a new one is hard work [...] The hours are long." He wrote and published a treatise, *ICONIC TREATISE GOTHIC FUTURISM*. In it, he seemed to be coding and decoding the everyday language around him, the speak of b-boy culture and graph writers, with a diaphanous relationship to time and reality. The continuum between graffiti writers and monks, digressions about the pope, and a war between letters were common themes in his tractate.

The artist became his own far-out sociohistorical authority on a kind of language with no father to its style, and its own orthography, writing impossible things. But it was not just an ideological project going on inside of the Battle Station: RAMM:ΣLL:ZΣΣ began to build a bricolaged army in his apartment, with Olde English brew sipped from a straw as his fuel, inside of a sarcophagus of fumes and glue, surrounded by masks, withdrawing more and more from the outside world into a world of letters.

RAMM:ΣLL:ZΣΣ, Clement writes in *Widow Basquiat*,

> says that he was put on Earth to smash the written word apart. He explains that all the letters of the English language come from social change, patriarchal societies, economics and history [...] He believes that the written letter in the Western alphabet is a reflection of a culture and philosophy that does not suit him or his brothers.

What the Martin case at large, and Rachel Jeantel's testimony more specificially, did was to materialize the war between languages that worried RAMM:ΣLL:ZΣΣ so much. When the trial was over and the verdict was in, the word "justice" seemed to have different meanings to different people. The jury has spoken, officials in the government said. And collectively, people seemed to turn the question on them. Yes, we know that the jury has spoken. But we don't understand you, or them. Do you speak English?

SO: A TRAIN RACES BENEATH THE CITY, having been made into a vehicle of war, covered with signatures and symbols, it goes crosstown, downtown, taking with it the story of dystopia and crack cocaine, "armamentation," and innovation as it travels. This is what myths do: they tell us how things came to be. And all too often the myth-making process is the only way people on the margins can "speak themselves" into existence. In her memoir, *Belonging: A Culture of Place* (1989), bell hooks writes, "It is the telling of our history that enables political self-recovery." The chance to reconfigure one's self, even if only in folklore or strange space lore, or on three whole cars, is an understandably provocative ability. We tell things these ways to warn against what hooks calls "forgetfulness." There is a Gothic saga, from the first century AD, that tells a story of migration and exodus, and these are its final lines:

> They went so far that they came to the land of the Greek [...] They settled there, and love there still, and still have something of our language.

In that same way, black Americans are conceived from a people whose fates, identities, and woes were decided by a doorway, and only a strange saga with strange letters can say how.

Those who were taken walked through that doorway and were told they had become something different from those who stayed behind, and in some ways they had. They forgot many things, and wondered how their mouths and muscles remembered things for them: recipes, movements, and stories. They crossed an ocean so still and so wide they must have imagined they had left earth and ended up elsewhere. Like all lost mariners, they learned to become astronomers, they kept their eyes on the gourd. When they landed they heard the word, Animals. And they thought, No, Aliens. ✦

FATHER-TO-BE TAKES HIMSELF FOR A WALK

DOUGLAS KEARNEY

out!
the final hospital stay's a leash,
so I'm bound to the bed N lay a week in,
weak to the *beep* of her flashflood blood
run these mudslide years of red.
I scratch at the window like some mutt
the night before strangers dump the trash.

N's a shotgun aimed at us.

come dawn, her doctor pulls her trigger,
bucks me into *Father*.
my stomach guards my wilting cock,
snarls at trespassing clocks.
N gnaws her steepled fingers.
I leave her there for food.

beg!
a fucked week sick with Korean burritos:
half-breed comida muk-da'ing my withering wallet.
that food truck chuckles to the hospital's lot,
"his parking stubs *stay* at daily max!"

damn I am tonight too mutt
for kalbi, kimchee, tomatillo,
I'm full of what I don't comprendo -
but dusk's a bloody chuck patty on the greasy griddle sky.
the stars: they sizzle. they pop.

heel!
walking west 6th, my shadow shies from MacArthur Park's heat and shivs.
not me though!
these new mongrel senses
are open wounds in lemon-tinted storefronts.

but what's it to know when today come yesterday
I'll no longer not be a father?
so long as tomorrow is tomorrow
and yesterday's yesterday
stays nearer to the bloody years of not knowing -

yet I'm not long for what I've been so long
and so near to what I'm going to,
tonight I am just a man and not quite
a father so nearly not just a man
and so?

babbling shopglass of bright ads, my reflection halved,
all I can't read as I pass.

down!
my eyes sic the bustling Food 4 Less.
my pissant shadow rank as a cur's piss.
I pack no pistol, speak no Spanish:
what future? unborn names sud my black-ass lips,
my heart a red dick out my head's hairy sheath.
my own dick abuts my haunch.
somebody put me down!

down a side street:
overgrown terraces calamitous with foreignness.

swearing the curbed cars are explosions
fixing to be cut out themselves, I'm down
the street's dividing line, my nose busted
with cumin, menudo, cinnamon.

speak!
I die at dawn, so I set to prowl
the mongrel hours God's silvered eye
hounds fools and children. stupid, childish
man's heart pump no Kool Aid, though!
I bark at near dark: *who wants some?!*
I could upchuck my lupine alarm at sudden blood.

but with sun comes soon some new tether to hitch my throat
and stifle now knee even now pants now
shook and up now stand now
dawn now these dull teeth
say the names, boy. speak!

THIS PAGE
FROM *POETRY: SORROW*, XEROX PRINT SET. 1965–1966

OPPOSITE PAGE
COFFIN: TIME PIECE: YELLOW ROSE, 1966
COURTESY OF THE GETTY RESEARCH INSTITUTE, LOS ANGELES

BARBARA T. SMITH

Though she's primarily known as a performance artist whose work has dealt explicitly with questions of feminism, ritual, spirituality, food, and the body, Barbara T. Smith also has a long history of making books. The following images and interview center on a particularly fevered, prolific period between 1965 and 1966 when she leased a Xerox machine in her home. Among the first artist books she ever made, the Xerox works employ the mechanical possibilities of the photocopy process to both inventive and acutely personal ends (Smith, a mother of three, found herself on the precipice of divorce during this time, her family life threatening to disintegrate); they also foreshadow some of the concerns that would re-emerge later in Smith's performances. Selections from Smith's Xerox books were recently shown at the Box Gallery in Los Angeles and have been acquired by the J. Paul Getty Museum.

KATE WOLF

BARBARA T. SMITH:
I had gone to Pomona College and got a great art history education there, part of which was about printmaking. In 1960, I started working as a volunteer at the Pasadena Art Museum and they had me working in the print collection. I learned firsthand about the conserving of prints and how to evaluate them. With etching and engravings especially, the big thing is not just the print itself, but whether you have an early print. In lithographs that's not as much an issue, because the stone doesn't deteriorate in the same way, but still, in Europe, they would print and print and print — they didn't destroy the master. Here, when they do an edition (it used to be on a stone or, later, a zinc plate) once the edition is done they destroy it, but they don't do that in Europe, so you can still have prints being made today of things by someone like Matisse.

I was learning about all of this, and I had an idea for a great print. (The idea was that you'd have the lithographic stone and then there'd be this kind of gravestone; I was going to make stone on stone. And then I was going to sandwich in between this a real lily, so it'd be this life sandwiched between death, or some such thing.) I knew about June Wayne, who had started a whole resurgence of lithography in the United States. Lithography had basically died — there were no master printers that anyone knew of, no place you could go. June was interested in lithography, so she began to research if there was anyone left in America who knew how to do it. She found printers around the country, and she brought them to Los Angeles, and started the Tamarind Lithography Workshop in 1960. She began to publish material about the art of lithography that circulated in the art world, especially the museums; she revived the entire art in this country. And then the printers who had worked with her went out into the world and helped start places like Gemini G.E.L.

I'd heard about all of this, and I met June and got the publications, and then I heard about Gemini. This was in 1965 or 1966. I didn't know anything about Gemini except that it was a printmaking place. So I went to their office, which was on Melrose, and I told them my name and that I would like to make a print there. And they sort of gulped and looked askance and said, "Well, it's customary for an artist who works here to have a gallery, and currently Josef Albers is working here, and he won't be through for quite a while."

I was really kind of outraged, partly not deserving to be, but I was. After, I was driving home and thinking, lithography isn't the printmaking medium of our time! It's 19th century; it's Daumier. So what is the printmaking medium of our era? *Business machines.* It just stimulated one thing after another. So then I thought — since I knew

TOP
FROM *POETRY: CHILD VOICE*, XEROX PRINT SET. 1965–1966

BOTTOM
GOD'S BREATH, 1965–1966
PHOTO CREDIT: FREDERIK NILSEN

HOOD ORNAMENT. 1965-1966
PHOTO CREDIT: FREDERIK NILSEN

the technology from both school and the Pasadena Museum — it has to be a different technology, a new technology. There were mimeograph and ditto machines, but that's all the same technology as lithographs. It's called "planer." The surface of the paper picks up the image: it doesn't bite into the paper; it's on the plane of the paper. In etching and engraving, it's on a plate that stamps hard and stamps the image into the paper, and that's called "intaglio."

So then I thought, well, how are all these new machines made? I started calling up printing places and asking what kind of process they used and the only one that was truly different was Xerox. Because the Xerox uses toner, which are tiny little beads of plastic. And it uses an electronically charged plate. It's photographic, in a way. Light travels underneath and picks up the image, like in television: every spot there's a dark place, there's dots; it copies that exactly. The image is sintered onto the paper. It melts the tiny beads of plastic into the page. The process is very carefully controlled: it's exactly hot enough to melt the beads without setting the paper on fire. But sometimes it still did; you just had reach in there and pull it out real quick.

I looked into how expensive it would to be to lease a Xerox machine. And once I got it, it was just dynamite. I just could not stop working on it, it was so much fun. From

INSTALLATION VIEW FROM *XEROX: BARBARA T. SMITH 1965 – 1966*. THE BOX, LOS ANGELES, CA
PHOTO CREDIT: FREDERIK NILSEN

then on, I fell into a kind of never-never land of creativity. It was like people who write a book: they start out way on the periphery and then they suddenly get into it and they're locked and they can't get out until it's finished. It was kind of like that. It kept leading me on, and it was just endless. The thing is that it's so responsive. If I had an idea, I could immediately see if it worked, whereas in the other kinds of art, you make a painting and either have to change it or throw it away; there's a length of time to make something happen. But with the Xerox stuff, I was just cranking it out.

You know how there's this story about the saltcellar at the bottom of the sea that won't stop putting out salt? I don't know the rest of the story, but that was the really scary part to me, that it just won't stop, and that's kind of what I felt like. It went on for months. And the Xerox machine is like a car; it needs servicing periodically. I could tell that it was due for servicing, because it started having these artifacts on the image. I saw this service was going to have to happen and that would disrupt everything I was trying to do, so I kept going and finally I was just completely dismayed. I said to Allen, my husband, "How am I going to stop this?" And he said, "Well, just call them up and tell them to come and get it." So that's what I did. I had maybe two weeks or however long to just jam, jam, jam, and try to finish everything. I realized then that

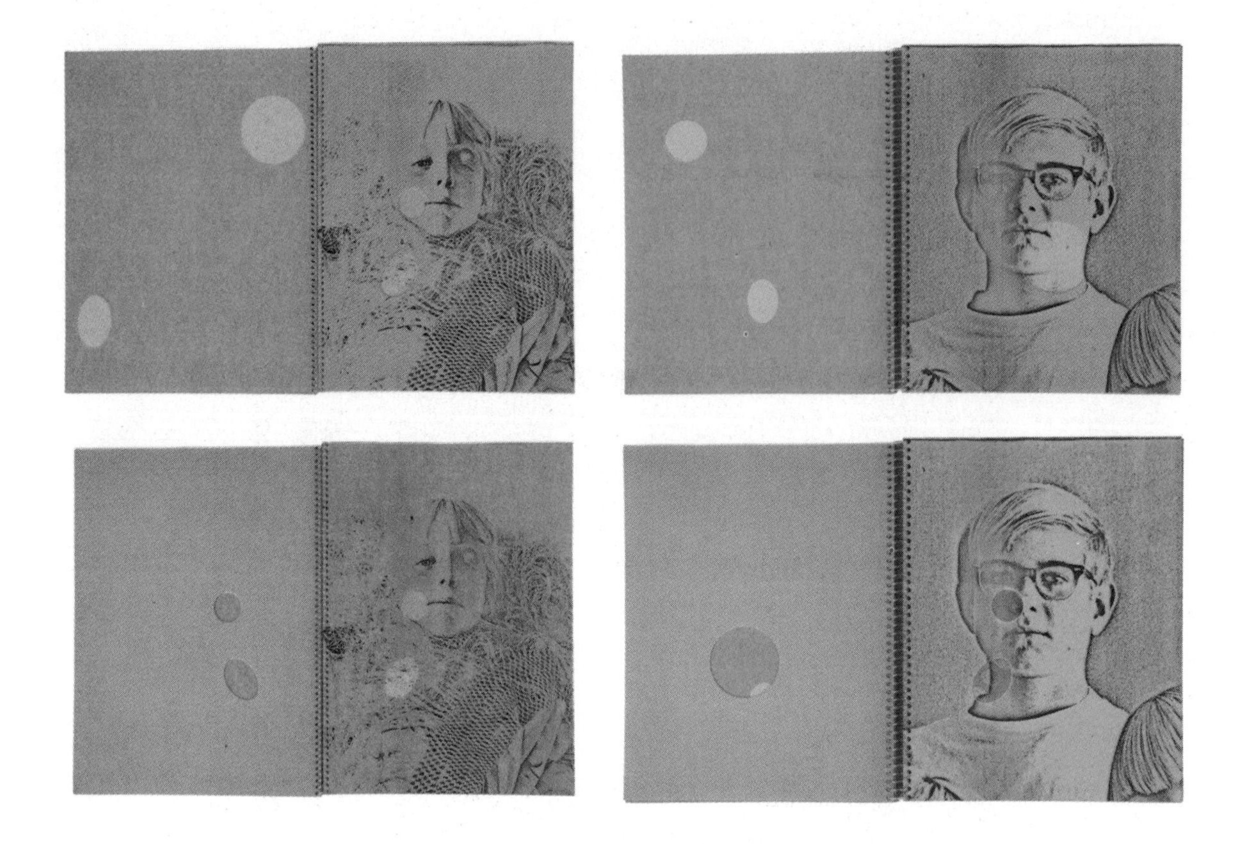

all the ideas I had originally started out with I'd never gotten a chance to do, so I started trying to do those, too. But that was very funny to me, that I had all these preconceived ideas, and they just went out the door.

Around the same time, I had the sense that my marriage was coming apart, but I really couldn't face it; I couldn't deal with it at all. But, being encapsulated by this process, I went and had Jerry McMillan photograph my children in particular ways and then another friend photographed me, and they were all for images for the books. My husband was an investment counselor and he had a lot of stocks and bonds, so he would get dividend checks in the mail and I made collages with the envelopes; I sometimes put those through the machine several times. Coming out of the envelopes there would be these little images, like children's stickers, and also images of my children. What I was actually doing in this was trying to entice my children out of the captivity of the corporate world, to elicit fun with those little toy things. I was just saying, "Come on out of there and be free!"

THIS PAGE

FROM *POETRY: XEROX, COFFIN, DIE CUT, JULIE HARD-BOUND*, 1965–1966
XEROX ARTIST BOOK, SPIRAL BOUND
9 X 11.25 INCHES

OPPOSITE PAGE, CLOCKWISE

XEROX, COFFIN, DIE CUT, KATIE HARD-BOUND, 1965-1966
XEROX ARTIST BOOK, SPIRAL BOUND
9 X 11.25 INCHES

XEROX, COFFIN, DIE CUT, KATIE HARD-BOUND, 1965-1966
XEROX ARTIST BOOK, SPIRAL BOUND
9 X 11.25 INCHES

XEROX, COFFIN, DIE CUT, RICK HARD-BOUND, 1965-1966
XEROX ARTIST BOOK, SPIRAL BOUND
9.75 X 14.25 INCHES

XEROX, COFFIN, DIE CUT, RICK HARD-BOUND, 1965-1966
XEROX ARTIST BOOK, SPIRAL BOUND
9.75 X 14.25 INCHES

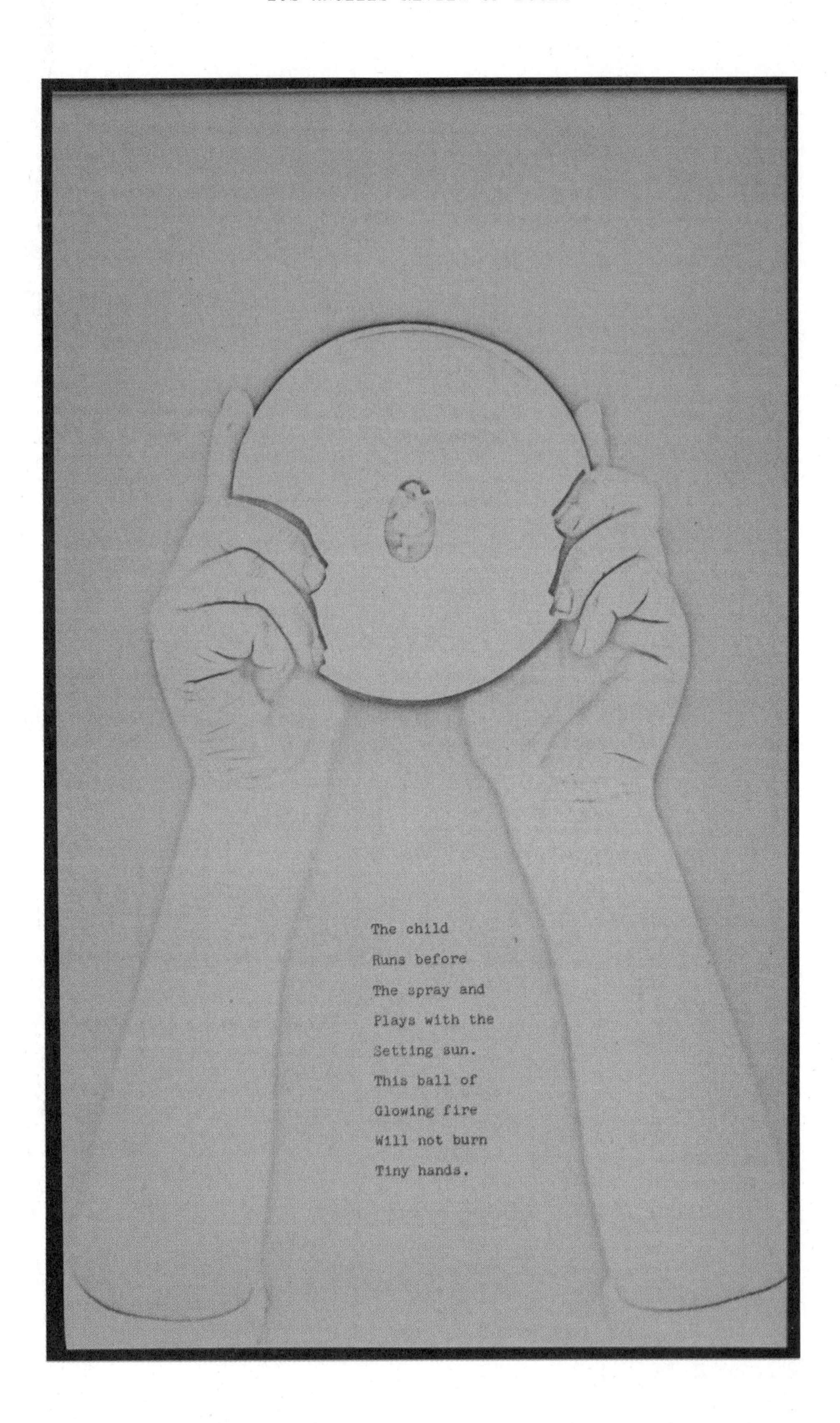
The child
Runs before
The spray and
Plays with the
Setting sun.
This ball of
Glowing fire
Will not burn
Tiny hands.

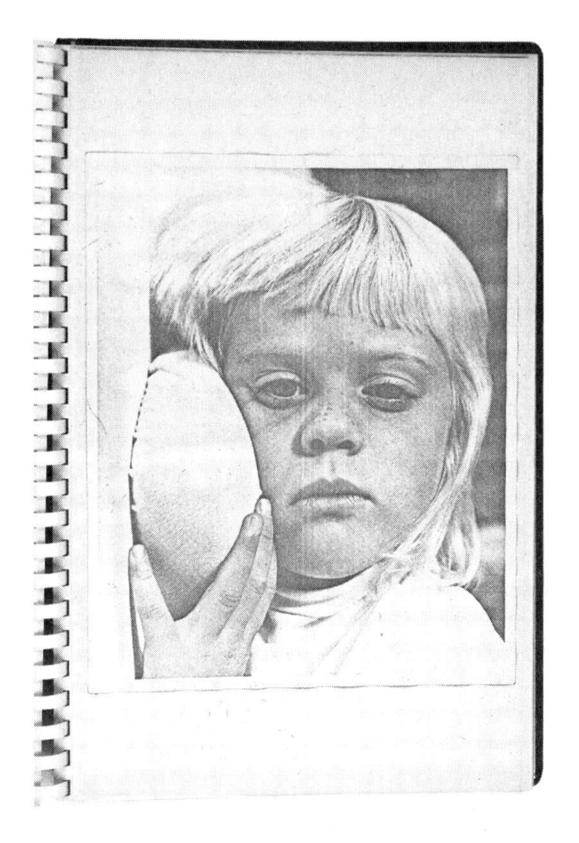

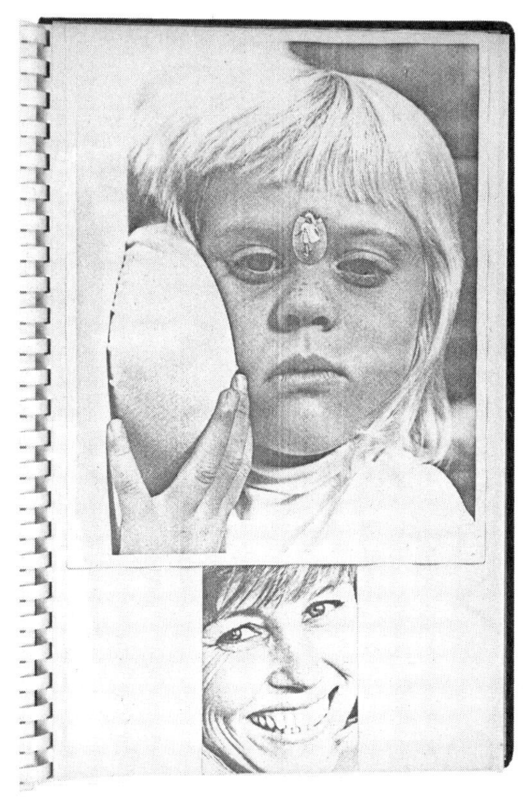

THIS PAGE | *XEROX, COFFIN, ENTHEOS.* 1965-1966
OPPOSITE PAGE | *POETRY: CHILD VOICE.* XEROX PRINT SET. 1965-1966

I began to see this series of books as coffins, as the end of something. All of them have a logo, a cross in a circle that's embossed on the center of the cover, and some have die-cut pages with holes. From my point of view, these ones with my children in them are about me trying to tell them that ultimately nothing is going to take them away from our relationship and despite the impending crisis they would be safe. The coffin resonates with my upbringing because my father was a funeral director. On that whole side of the family — my father was a mortician, my grandfather was, my great uncles were, my uncle, my brother, my mother — they all worked in the mortuary. So coffins were familiar. On a certain energetic level, I'm aware of a continuum of death; I mean, it's sad and dark, but it's not terrible: it's what is. But coffins are definite ends — the end. And I was just like a mesmerized person then, and I realized, these books were coffins. ✦

THE NIGHT STALKER

ALEX ESPINOZA

On May 29, 1985, Richard Ramirez entered the home of two elderly sisters and beat them with a hammer. One survived; on the other's shattered body and bedroom walls, Ramirez scrawled pentagrams with a tube of lipstick. The next day, he raped, sodomized, and slashed a middle-aged woman before tying her to her 12-year-old son.

It was my 14th birthday.

We lived in the shadow of Los Angeles, in cities perpetually veiled in a brown haze that turned the sun a rusty orange. We were immigrants from Mexico, Guatemala, El Salvador, the Philippines. With the rest of Reagan's America, we shared fears of AIDS, of atomic bombs, of Armageddon. But there, in the San Gabriel Valley, we also feared unemployment and unpaid mortgages, unwanted pregnancies, drug addiction, and gang violence. A serial killer haunting our suburban streets, though, was a menace for which we had never prepared.

Each morning that summer, we watched the news, waiting to learn who hadn't survived the night. Names. Ages. Cities where my friends lived, streets I'd traveled, buildings I recognized. Images of bloody sheets and busted doors. We wondered when the Night Stalker would come for us. We armed ourselves with guns and baseball bats. My uncle bought my aunt a machete. Our mailman gave my mother a can of mace. My sisters took self-defense classes. My brothers sparred with one another inside our garage. We reinforced our doors and windows, sealing ourselves from both danger and the cool night air. Lying in my bedroom, so very hot and still, I remember thinking, "This is what a coffin must feel like."

Then, in late August, Ramirez was spotted in East L.A. A group of residents chased him down, beat him, and held him for the police. And so it ended.

There was no recognizable pattern to the attacks, no modus operandi. His victims were male and female, young and old, white and Asian, African-American and Latino. They were people our blue-collar communities recognized. They worked alongside our fathers, went to our schools, shopped at the stores our mothers did. The fear we experienced that summer was real. We knew it would linger long after his capture.

When he was convicted in 1989, Richard Ramirez addressed the courtroom: "I am beyond good and evil. I will be avenged. Lucifer dwells in us all."

We believed him then. After all this time, we still do.

To The Lighthouse

ARIANA KELLY

I dream of living in a lighthouse
The white one by the bay
So if you want to make my dreams come true
You'll be a lighthouse keeper too

Erika Eigen
"I Want to Marry a Lighthouse Keeper"

Robert Louis Stevenson was a great disappointment to his father. Although he would become the author of such canonical novels as *Treasure Island* and *The Strange Case of Dr. Jekyll and Mr. Hyde,* Thomas Stevenson never completely forgave him for refusing to follow in the Stevenson tradition of becoming a lighthouse engineer. His grandfather was the second engineer for the Northern Lighthouse board established in 1796 — he succeeded his stepfather — and quickly became famous throughout Britain for lighting what had been a coastal Desolation Row. The work suited his penchant for solitude and for adventure, and each of his sons strove to continue and improve his legacy so that by 1850, when the future writer was born, the name Stevenson had become synonymous with lighthouses. "You have rendered my whole life a failure," Stevenson the elder informed his son in 1873, even though it was clear that much of his son's work, and life, would be inspired by the wrecks lighthouses strove to prevent.

The first prototypes of lighthouses were bonfires built on elevated land, or even,

RON REGÉ, JR.

some speculate, on top of Sumerian ziggurats. As ports developed, the elevations became manmade and the fires enclosed. Two of the earliest lighthouses, the Pharos of Alexandria and the Colossus of Rhodes, were among the Seven Wonders of the World. The Colossus of Rhodes — a statue of the Titan Helios holding a light — was the principal inspiration for the Statue of Liberty (which was, between 1886–1901, maintained by the United States Lighthouse Board).

Rather than serving as warnings to prevent ships from running aground, early lighthouses were placed at the entrances of harbors to conduct them in. Fueled by various materials such as wood, coal, candles, and, finally, oil, the light provided by lighthouses remained notoriously dim even as their assistance became more and more important. In the late 1700s, mirrors placed around the light source were partially effective in reflecting and thereby intensifying the light. Still, even the best mirrors lost half their illumination to absorption, and most lost even more due to surface flaws in the glass.

A dark coast could be deadly. In 1816, over 300 ships were recorded as having vanished or wrecked. In all likelihood the numbers were much greater. One of the most infamous of these disasters was immortalized by the painter Theodore Géricault in *The Raft of the Medusa* (1818–1819). In July of 1816 *la Méduse* struck the Bank of Arguin, an almost completely unlit section of the African coast. The ship's few lifeboats could not accommodate all of the fleeing passengers, and the remainder constructed an unwieldy raft of planks, masts, and rope. Fifteen days later, most of the passengers were dead, and the fifteen who survived did so only by eating the remains of their companions. The account of the experience written by two survivors enthralled the public and inspired Géricault's painting.

During the same week that the then-unknown Géricault displayed *The Raft of the Medusa* at the Paris Salon, Augustin Fresnel presented his design for a lens that would intensify the brightness emitted from a traditional lighthouse, although he was met with a much more skeptical reception than Géricault. By this time Fresnel — the hero of Theresa Levitt's new book *A Short Bright Flash: Augustin Fresnel and the Birth of the Modern Lighthouse* — was already a connoisseur of light, having spent years trying to prove that light behaved as a wave, not a particle, as Newton concluded. Fresnel's insight was to replace mirrors with lenses. Rather than intensifying light by reflecting it, a lens could magnify light by bending it, gathering all of the illumination from a single origin and consolidating it into one beam. This solution still presented problems: in order to refract as much light as possible the light needed to be bent as sharply as possible, which required a thicker lens that, frustratingly, lost light. Fresnel's solution was the dioptric (refractive) lens for which he became famous. Constructed in steps, the lens broke "the single curved surface into several concentric sections consisting of distinct prisms, or triangular prisms of glass that would refract the light." Each of these individual prisms would "bend the light rays from their source into a parallel line." This innovation alone allowed Fresnel illuminations to far surpass any of his competitors', but it was his design for a lens that utilized both reflection and refraction — the catadioptric lens — that was to be his crowning accomplishment, albeit one only realized after his death of tuberculosis at the age of 39.

LEVITT'S BOOK IS THE FIRST SERIOUS ATTEMPT to trace the evolution of the modern lighthouse, focusing specifically on Fresnel's innovations and the "intersection of empire, science, and engineering" that made them possible. She describes Fresnel, a Jansenist and a Royalist until he died, as the image of "northern phlegmatic self-possession," but encounters with the lens he created are usually described in the language of awe reserved for natural or spiritual phenomena. To see it is to be reminded that Fresnel literally bent light to do his bidding. "In the middle of the chamber was the light itself," the contemporary artist Peter Hill writes of first seeing a Fresnel lens, "like the giant eyeball of a one-eyed God. [...] I stared at it in wonder. It was like being close to a sleeping wild animal with no bars in-between." Indeed, one of the most arresting moments in Levitt's book occurs in the preface, when she describes encountering, as a young girl, the "strange, glittering contraption" on the top floor of the Alaska State Museum:

> The hundreds of finely polished prisms placed into a precise but inscrutable pattern gave it an unworldly effect, especially when you have just emerged from the wilds of the boreal forest. The unusual design of the lens, including its sharply peaked top, made it look like a spaceship that had accidentally touched down in Alaska.

My own first encounter with a Fresnel lens occurred recently, at the Cabrillo State Monument, a state park at the southern tip of the Point Loma peninsula in San Diego, an area otherwise dominated by the military. (There are, in fact, two lighthouses on Point Loma, the original built in 1854 and closed in 1891 because its 461-foot elevation, initially a source of some fame, meant that it was routinely shrouded in marine layer, and then its replacement, which stands, rocket-like and unapproachable, much closer to the shore.) The Fresnel lens sits safely enclosed in a special area adjacent to the original keeper's quarters, which have been restored and turned into a museum. The day I was there, a gaggle of young children pawed at the glass, as interested by the system of weights used to turn the lens as they were by the lens itself. Flanked by numerous informational plaques to tell us what we were seeing, and why it was important, I was reminded not so much of a one-eyed God but of Rilke's panther, whose "vision, from the constantly passing bars, / has grown so weary that it cannot hold / anything else."

The effectiveness of the Fresnel lens, not to mention the work required to make it, made lighthouses symbols not of isolation but of connection. "Among the most difficult pieces of technology developed in the 19th century," according to Levitt, the Fresnel lens "push[ed] at the edges of what was physically possible." Fresnel's ambition to light the coast required the mass production of high quality glass as well as traditional craftsmanship to shape this glass. All of France was utilized to illuminate the sea.

THE OLD POINT LOMA LIGHTHOUSE was one of six commissioned for California in 1850, just 19 days after California was recognized as a state. For a long time, while the shores of Europe, Asia, and Africa were illuminated by the Fresnel lens, America's coastline had remained curiously dark. In the early 19th century, Levitt asserts, the nascent country's ingenuity and energy were not yet supported by the educational system required to realize its visions. The country's youth and inexperience were only exacerbated by an unenlightened head of the US Treasury Department's Lighthouse Establishment, Stephen Pleasonton, who saw little value in the Fresnel lenses and refused to spend the comparatively large amount of money needed to purchase them. In the 1840s and 1850s, however, thinkers like Henry David Thoreau, Herman Melville, and Walt Whitman spurred an intellectual revolution that facilitated technological growth and strengthened the country's infrastructure. Each of these people perceived lighthouses as symbols of progress and innovation.

America's commitment to building more lighthouses and improving those already existing coincided with a massive territorial expansion; in just a few years the total length of its coastline doubled. Lighthouse technology developed in tandem with that of the railroad and telegraph, all of which allowed people to communicate over the long distances that would come to characterize America and modern life in general. Once gold was discovered in 1848, the need for lighthouses increased exponentially as the California coast became an epicenter of global commerce. California went on to establish 21 lighthouses along its coastline. Weeks after gold was discovered in the Klondike region of Alaska, Levitt notes, the government purchased 11 Fresnel lenses. By 1856, the United States possessed more lighthouses than any other "developed sea-faring nation" and they went on to play pivotal roles for both the Union and Confederate armies. All of this supports Levitt's contention that "[t]he moment a Fresnel lens appeared at a location was the moment the region became linked to the world economy."

The more sophisticated lighthouses became, the more they were militarized. It was common practice for colonialists to mark a new territory by building a lighthouse. During the Civil War, both the Union and Confederate armies made significant gains and suffered significant losses according to their possession or loss of specific lighthouses. "On April 19, 1861," Levitt writes, "as his first official act of war, Lincoln ordered a blockade of the Southern coast, divided between an Atlantic and a Gulf blockade. The South responded by putting out all lights in its lighthouses." Fresnel lenses went on to be stolen, vandalized, or sometimes completely destroyed.

In the 20th century, the exigencies of World War I necessitated the transfer of American lighthouses from civilian to military jurisdiction so that they could be used for surveillance. At the end of the war, supervision returned to the Lighthouse Service, only to be removed again, with World War II looming, this time by President Roosevelt, who entrusted their administration to the coast guard. Roosevelt continued the process of automation that had begun in 1919. Eventually, the galactic lenses that hung like giant chandeliers and weighed thousands of pounds were replaced with quartz-iodine, high-intensity lamps weighing perhaps 20 pounds, run on electricity and operated remotely. While lighthouses played a pivotal role during World War II — the day after the bombing of Pearl Harbor the entire American coastline went dark — the war effort had spurred governments to redouble their research into radio and sonar navigation in the attempt to eliminate margins of error. With the advent of global positioning systems, we became able to pinpoint our locations and chart our trajectories with near-miraculous perfection and to do so with little to no human aid. Keepers had once been necessary to fuel the lights, clean the lenses, and wind the clocks, but by the millennium, they were all but obsolete.

IN THE 19TH CENTURY, according to Levitt, lighthouses were nexus points of scientific, political, and cultural revolution. By the end of the 20th, they were symbols of romantic isolation and withdrawal. Of course, the lighthouse keeper had always been a solitary figure. In the last months of his life Edgar Allan Poe, who died just before Robert Louis Stevenson was born, began work on an untitled story unofficially known as "The Lighthouse." Set in 1796 and told in a series of diary entries (there are only four and the last consists simply of a date), the narrator alternately celebrates and regrets his isolation: "My spirits are beginning to revive already," he writes on January 1, "at the mere thought of being — for once in my life at least — thoroughly alone." Just a few lines later he meditates on the gloominess of the word *alone*: "I could half fancy there was some peculiarity in the echo of these cylindrical walls — but oh, no! — this is all nonsense. I do believe I am going to get nervous about my isolation." By January 3, the date of the last complete entry, he has begun to question the solidity of the lighthouse's foundation and its ability to withstand the winds and high-running seas.

In 1999, in my last year of college, I harbored dreams of becoming a lighthouse keeper. What attracted me was partly what attracted Poe: the solitary nature of the work. It was a job akin to being a fire lookout, or a forest ranger, positions that require a capacity, if not a desire, for isolation. But it was also work whose demands and usefulness are immediately clear. "I can think of no other edifice constructed by man," wrote George Bernard Shaw, "as altruistic as a lighthouse." It is a light lit for the sake of others. The first lighthouse keepers were usually slaves or soldiers, but by the Middle Ages many of the tenders were monks and nuns who viewed the position not so much as a job but as an opportunity to serve, and the lighthouse itself a symbol of spiritual aspiration. After Henry VIII dissolved the monasteries in the first half of the 16th century, keepers became a much more motley crew. By the early 1900s, when Shaw was writing, over 500 civilian lighthouse keepers operated and maintained over 800 lighthouses in the United States alone. Many of the civilian keepers were keepers because they liked and needed the work; others were there because they wanted the life experience a more conventional job might not afford. In both cases they rendered services, in the popular imagination at least, beyond those of tending the light.

I discovered soon enough, however, that I was too late to join this exalted company. In 2000, Congress passed the National Historic Preservation Act, sanctioning the transfer of lighthouses to eligible "federal or state agencies, local governments, and nonprofit groups." The lighthouse keeper had become not an altruist but a preservationist, a protector not of lives but of memories.

"How is it that our memories seem to be made of lights?" asks Thomas Dolby in his 2013 documentary *The Invisible Lighthouse*. Dolby, an English composer and producer best known for his 1982 hit single "She Blinded Me with Science," grew up and currently lives on what he describes as the "anxious" coast of East Anglia, in sight of the Orford lighthouse. "From my earliest memories," Dolby told me, "I remember falling sleep with the light from the lighthouse flashing against my wall every five

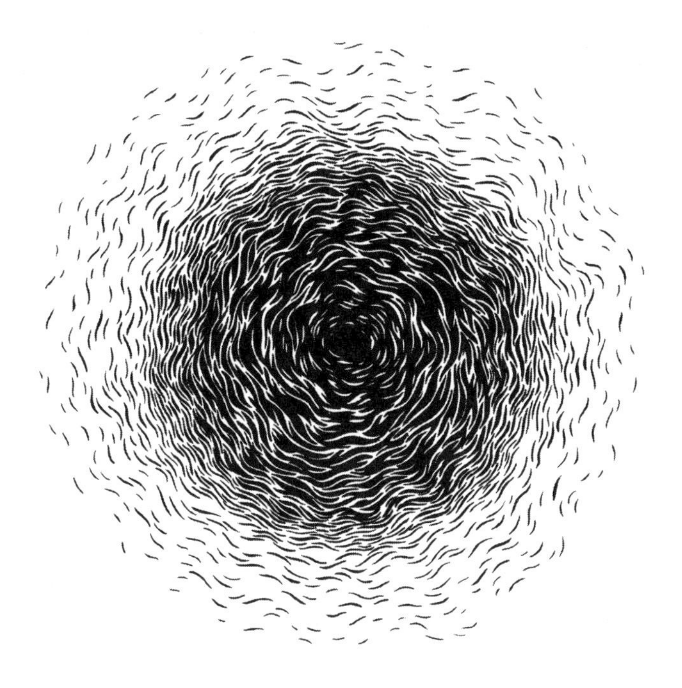

seconds." The Orford lighthouse was erected in 1792 on what is now an ex-military island that was decommissioned at the end of June, according to Dolby, "partly because there's less call to use lighthouses for navigation now. And partly because there's very bad erosion along this coast, and the lighthouse has lost a lot of beach in front of it." In fact, as Dolby says, because of rising sea levels, the British Isles "are tipping eastward," and the fear was that the lighthouse would eventually collapse, releasing all of its hazardous materials with it. "On a certain level it makes me incredibly sad," Dolby continues, "but there was never really a movement to preserve it." Instead the decommissioned lighthouse will be detoxified and then left to erode. To some extent, Dolby's film is itself an effort at preservation, not just of the lighthouse but of the entire area, which is, he says, "slowly but surely tipping into the North Sea," going the same way as the lighthouse. "The lighthouse is the fulcrum," Dolby says of *The Invisible Lighthouse*, but "it's really about memory." Referred to as the "British Roswell" due to an alleged UFO sighting in 1980, the Orford Ness Island is a former military testing zone for experimental weapons; civilians are not allowed on site because it is littered with unexploded mines. When Dolby tried to find out when the lighthouse would be closed so that he could film it, he was told that this was classified information, and that it would be far too dangerous to be on the island unattended. He ignored the injunction and went out on a "daring commando raid," clandestinely filming footage with commercial cameras that he then learned how to

BRENDAN MONROE

edit himself. The result is impressionistic and atmospheric, less of a straightforward documentary and more, in Dolby's words, of a "tone poem."

Their privileged positions in personal and geographic landscapes have made lighthouses particularly vulnerable to sentimentality: for every actual lighthouse, there seem to be an infinite number of miniature replicas or calendar images. As Dolby says, every lighthouse is "somebody's pet." Though there are fewer actual working lighthouses with each passing year, the lighthouse has not lost its potency as a symbol.

In different ways, both Levitt and Dolby are trying to pierce the nostalgic haze that surrounds lighthouses without destroying the aura that makes them so resonant. "I've always thought these lighthouses are like stakes tethering the British Isles in place," one person commented in response to the trailer for Dolby's film. "As more and more are abandoned and fall to ruin, eventually we'll break free and either crash into Europe or drift across the Atlantic."

BEFORE HE DIED AT THE AGE OF 44, Robert Louis Stevenson traveled widely around the eastern and central Pacific Ocean. In 1889 he finally settled on the island of Samoa, where the tropical weather was good for his fragile health, and where he is buried in a tomb behind the island's old lighthouse.

"When darkness fell," Virginia Woolf writes in her 1927 novel *To the Lighthouse*, "the stroke of the Lighthouse, which had laid itself with such authority upon the carpet in the darkness, tracing its pattern, came now in the softer light of spring mixed with moonlight gliding gently as if it laid its caress and lingered stealthily and looked and came lovingly again." "Lovingly" is the key word in this passage. Unlike the radar, sonar, and satellite technologies that have replaced them, which track and triangulate us invisibly, lighthouses make themselves known to us, and thus make light personal. Out at sea, whatever that sea may be, you know that light is meant for you and for you alone. ✦

O TREE (BORASSUS)

HOA NGUYEN

Bud that chops the hill
I was there   I clock
foolish making a leaf soup

Napalm is a jellied gasoline

This makes sense: bombs &
the sappy will swings

"Wars are more fun with money"

Pine swung   oak-aloof
branch down   chainsaw down
Father burning the tent caterpillar nest

What do you see in the fire?

Isolated trees
Palmyra tree
Green bluish leaves

Claes Oldenburg
Writing on the Side
1956–1969

Note to Self: On Claes Oldenburg

ALEX KITNICK

Coming to realize my theme for the last two years has been my notes, or myself, or my facing up to self as intellectual and getting rid of disguise as baker, etc. The subject has been my own thought processes, my notes. Theme only becomes apparent now ... Publish notebooks.

Claes Oldenburg
1969

They put a great photograph on the cover of Claes Oldenburg's new book, *Writing on the Side, 1956–1969*, a collection of diary entries, poems, scripts, thoughts, and theories culled from the artist's most formative phase. An old typewriter is sitting on top of a wooden box atop a desk, paper rolled around the platen with a handful of words typed out. Above the typewriter, to the right, hangs an image of a saw outlined in black spray paint; a few file folders lie below. The photograph presents itself as a still life, but it's not the typical combination of artist's aids, like paint and brush or hammer and chisel that we see here. Rather, new combinations of things have taken shape. Typewriter and saw belong together; theory and practice inhabit the same space. One might even say they are conjoined: thinking is a physical activity and fabrication a theoretical one. One sees this in Oldenburg's sculpture as well. If not quite philosopher's stones, his lumpen sculptural forms — whether made of papier-mâché or sewn fabric — present themselves as thought objects, things that have been thought about, worried over, overtly (and overly) invested with feeling. With the publication of *Writing on the Side*, one is given a better sense of the artist's raw material: the thoughts and anxieties that went into his work.

FLOOR CONE (1962) IN FRONT OF DWAN GALLERY, LOS ANGELES, 1963. OLDENBURG VAN BRUGGEN STUDIO

The conceptual and the practical do not merge seamlessly, however. If theory and practice go hand in hand in Oldenburg's world, the cover photograph suggests that they are locked in struggle as well. The saw, looming like a phantom, slices across the sheet of paper while the brush at the bottom lies ready to sweep up the scraps.

Writing will be cut down to size, the photograph suggests, its instruments treated like so much raw material. Two years before this photograph was taken, in fact, in 1963, Oldenburg made *Soft Typewriter*, a dumb object that prohibits writing; later, in 1969, he made a drawing that serves up a slice of *Typewriter-Pie*. Perhaps even more to the point is a note that Oldenburg made in his journal in December 1966, which has the ring of both a sculptural procedure and a frustrated cry for help: "Fill typewriter with plaster. SHUT IT UP." This is sculpture as stoppage, an attempt to bring thought to a halt. (It is less an assisted readymade than an assaulted one.) Indeed, the influencing machine that is writing haunts all of Oldenburg's work, and at times he felt the need to fight against it. The typewriter functioned as a symbol of this productive anxiety. If the typewriter put Oldenburg to work, sometimes it also had to be put in its place, which is to say that it had to be treated ruthlessly and mercilessly, like a thing among others.

AT THE BEGINNING OF *WRITING ON THE SIDE*, Oldenburg often wonders whether he is a painter or a sculptor. He is both, of course. But, since the beginning of his career, he has always been a writer, too, and not just a writer but someone obsessed with writing, with written and printed matter, with papery things and their location in space. For Oldenburg, writing was not simply a mental activity but a *thing* to do; his goal was to make writing thing-like. "The writing I do is affected by the same emphasis on visual and tactile — the sensuous element that has produced my peculiar kind of theater — of surfaces, of form, of images, of color, and without words," he writes in 1966. "I type because it's the most physical way of writing":

> I play the typewriter like I used to play the drums. I stand when I type, because that way I feel body, space, and movement. The meaning of my writing is often in the sound rather than the idea, as it would be in the surface of paint rather than in the subject. My literary effects, if any, consist of stringing together images. I analyzed this once because I wanted to become a writer. I found that I was not a writer because I could not proceed horizontally, only spatially.

If sculpture ultimately lent itself to Oldenburg's spatial inclinations more than writing did (he had originally sought to be a journalist), the latter occupation continued to play a key role in his practice even if he often strove to picture it as something else. Indeed, Oldenburg is often at pains to downplay writing's role in his process. "My studio notes are more of a way of expelling stupid thoughts," he tells himself in 1965–66. They allow "me to continue with my work." A few stanzas later he adds: "I am embarrassed by my public statements because they are attributed to *me* ... or to a fictional character, 'Claes Oldenburg,' I'd really prefer to change ... but who is expected to show consistency." Less an objection to writing per se than an anxiety about the uses to which writing is put, Oldenburg's main concern is about speaking for his objects. He doesn't want to offer up a solid "Claes Oldenburg" that would stand firmly behind his production. His notes-to-self served a different function, however; they helped him navigate his activities and test the differences between words and things. (This is why, by 1969, he instructs himself to "publish notebooks.") They also helped him get words into things. Frequently, however, and especially at the beginning of his career, language erupts in Oldenburg's work as a subject in itself.

Writing on the Side, a big unannotated tome that I imagine will be of most use to scholars and Oldenburg diehards, was published on the occasion of the MoMA exhibition *Claes Oldenburg: The Street and The Store*, which focused on two of the artist's key projects from the early 1960s in which language played a central role. *Empire Sign – With M and I Deleted* (1960) is a first hint at the dialectical play with information and noise that will continue throughout Oldenburg's work. Crafted from papier-mâché, a primary material for Oldenburg in these years, and hanging off the wall like the sign to a dingy hotel or bar, the work pictures language as twice decayed: it falls apart on the level of both spelling and structure. Though one can still deduce the word-referent in *Empire Sign*, afterward very little language is legible. Two *Street Signs* from the same year possess similarly sharp contours of jagged yet droopy lettering (they look almost like limbs), but offer little decipherable information. A small sculpture titled *Letter Tenement* (1960), a bandaged edifice covered in similarly melted lettering, is equally difficult to read. Words don't communicate here; they are simply stuff — "heaps of language" as Robert Smithson would later remark. "Most of what people say is noise anyway," Oldenburg writes, "and actual speech appears meaningless, f.ex., verbatim press conferences." Oldenburg's linguistic breakdown not only mimed the physical condition of the postwar New York in which the artist lived; it also articulated what he saw as the impoverishment of speech around him, its tendency toward banality and instrumentalization. No wonder that every time we see a human figure in one of his drawings, the accompanying speech balloon is empty.

"Lonely in new city — interested in people — outside experience," Oldenburg writes just after moving to New York in 1956. Living in the East Village he soon finds company by using the city as material: "My stuff is made of what is around me — trumpets, bad music, gidoudahere, whistles, car honks ... ad information." The final item on Oldenburg's list suggests a Pop proclivity, but just as important are the sounds that lead up to it, which upbraid the typically smooth surfaces of Pop. (Ad information, after all, can be aural, too: think of radio jingles, or the saccharine sounds of ice cream trucks.) The street is where words assume physical presence, however, where they get turned into posters and signs, but it is also where they molder and fall prey to all manner of noise. Oldenburg made this well and clear in a series of anarchic performances at the Judson Square Church, dubbed *The Street*, in which he tore at a pile of soiled newspapers and emitted primal screams while bandaged in rags. (*The Street* sculptures on display at MoMA, it should be noted, first appeared at an exhibition at New York's Reuben Gallery two months later.)

If Oldenburg clobbered together words in his *Street* sculptures, in his writing of the time he was at pains to parse them out, to get his street head straight. He was nothing if not meticulous in the organization of his writing. He reflects frequently on his note-taking: "Monday, April 28, 1958: Redid notes. Classification, etc," he writes. A year later: "The notes in small books, pasted up and sorted and criticized, are taking the place of the speckled-book notes. This began in spring. Signifies and different process, attitude to notes." I could cite many more examples of Oldenburg noting notes, the way he watches himself moving between different methodologies of notation and organization. At one point he cuts his notes out and pastes them down on bigger sheets of paper, trying to find order in them, following something like the cut-up method of Brion Gysin and William Burroughs.

Like those writers, Oldenburg cut to analyze, to make sense, but he also wanted to give words presence as things. He did the same to images. He was always clipping and cutting out pictures of butter pats, olives, and cigarettes, and submitting them to analysis. In 1971, he published *Notes in Hand*, a collection of pocket-sized facsimiles of magazine clippings, "miniatures of my Notebook pages," paired with pages of typographical transcriptions that turn into Mallarméan poems. (Though these are omitted from *Writing on the Side*, we are treated to facsimiles of a host of other, similar notebook pages.) Here, we see images annotated as a photographer might mark prints. "Highlight here," "burn there," "overexposed." A number of pages include marginalia that add another view on the image, another rhyme; powdered milk spilled into coffee becomes "rainstorm at sea."

Though the basic structure resembles a scrapbook, these notes are not suffused with memory as much as they are made ready for manipulation. These advertising images, Oldenburg suggests, are manual devices; they can be cut out and taken hold of. One might even wrap one's head around them as well. But then what? Is comprehension enough? "Magazines — the contemporary reality," Oldenburg writes early on, in 1956, to which he quickly adds, "(to cut is to participate?)." This is the core question of Oldenburg's practice: how does one get involved with the things of this new pop world? Is cutting them out enough? Or is it too private an activity? Is cobbling together better? Would offering up readymades be okay? Or must one manipulate things? *How does one participate?* One hint at Oldenburg's solution to this problem is his insistence on working in public sites, not only in public plazas as he would beginning in the late 1960s, but in *The Street* as well. To participate means to make things public.

After *The Street*, Oldenburg moved on to *The Store*, a pseudo-Mom-and-Pop shop he set up on New York's Lower East Side in 1962, where common objects — a pair of sneakers, a hamburger, a case of pies — were rendered in a drippy Abstract Expressionist vernacular, as if a small factory had hired Jackson Pollock to put the finishing touches on its products. Here, Oldenburg's interest in language was put to a different test. If language broke down in *The Street*, in *The Store* it embodied itself in objects: the sculptures look like 3-D versions of the illustrations that accompany dictionary definitions. "The grossly mimetic character of" Oldenburg's work, the critic Bill Brown has written, functions "to theatricalize the point that all objects (not things) are first off iconic signs. (A sink looks like a sink.)" A close look at Oldenburg's crude rendering of such things in *The Store*, however, modifies Brown's point. His lesson, in fact, seems to be that *this* is not *that*, that objects can't be boiled down to words. When one

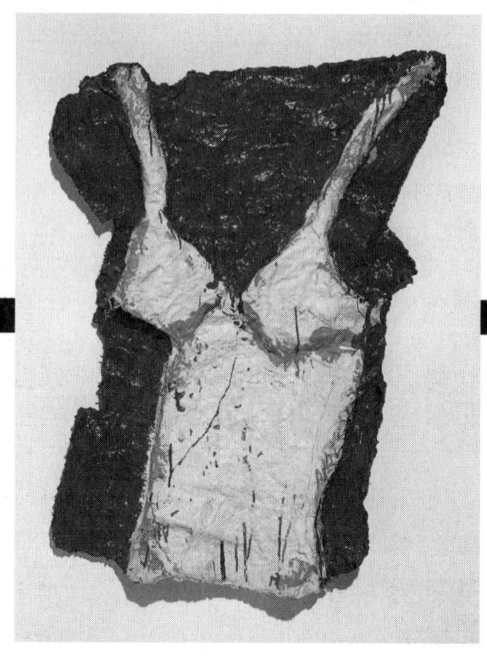

LEFT: *7-UP*. 1961. PHOTO: LEE STALSWORTH / RIGHT: *BRASELETTE*. 1961. PHOTO: DOUGLAS M. PARKER STUDIOS

boils down objects, in fact, one gets something much stranger than that with which one began.

Many of Oldenburg's artworks from this time lead far from static lives. They were made to be used. If categorization speaks to the museum's emphasis on stasis, performance puts objects to work. They were not objects to be looked at, but to be moved like props — one might even call them scripted. Over the course of *The Store*'s run, Oldenburg held a number of performances that incorporated his sculptures. Some of these scripts are included in *Writing on the Side*, but I prefer Oldenburg's *Raw Notes* (1973) — a book of thoughts and descriptions of these performances typed up one-sided like a movie script — as the proper testament. (Tellingly, the script for a work called *The Typewriter* appears in both volumes.) Marcel Duchamp's notes in his *Green Box* clearly served as inspiration here, but importantly Oldenburg's words were meant to work objects. Where Duchamp's notes provide a pile of hermeneutic possibilities, Oldenburg's function less as objects of encrypted inspiration than as a compendium of how-to instructions. If a readymade is made for the museum, an Oldenburg sculpture might find itself more comfortable onstage.

This talk of Duchamp brings us to Oldenburg's connections to the mainstream of 20th-century sculpture. His work has an undeniable purchase on the readymade, even if there is a sense that Oldenburg's objects are never fully ready, nor ever completely made: Oldenburg not only cut, tore, pasted, and scripted his work, but he put it into circulation as well. Recently, the curator Helen Molesworth has challenged the idea that the readymade dominated the 20th century by offering an account informed by the psychoanalyst Melanie Klein's theory of the part-object. She convincingly demonstrates that factory-produced work shared space with objects that ask to be sucked and fondled, and to which we cathect (the classic example of the part-object is the mother's breast). She cites Jasper Johns's sculpmetal lightbulbs, Eva Hesse's rubbery objects, and Robert Gober's wax legs, among others, as examples. Oldenburg should be included in this list, too, though his objects emerge less from a pre-lingual state than they do from a moment we might characterize as *after language*. Indeed, more than anything, Oldenburg's work speaks to the instrumentalization of language, and his struggle to work against it. This is why Oldenburg's work strikes us as so topical today: just as language is taking a new type of beating in the era of the hashtag, near-animate things and gadgets impinge on our space in increasingly novel ways.

Oldenburg, now an octogenarian, is still making work today, but *Writing on the Side* cuts off in 1969. In 1968, his notes begin to peter out. Perhaps personal-professional-political demands and preoccupations began to take their toll. It was around this time that he, along with his late wife Coosje van Bruggen, began to make the drab, larger-than-life sculptures that were subsequently foisted upon corporate lobbies and sculpture parks the world over. In September 1968 Oldenburg writes, "True, I don't talk to the typewriter as much anymore." A few months earlier, he reminds himself: "I must not forget the incredible pleasures of typewriting." Nevertheless, his writing soon slips away. *Writing on the Side* serves as a reminder not only of the pleasures of typing, but of the perils we face when we go without. ✦

A Man Who Has Come Through: On D.H. Lawrence

MARJORIE PERLOFF

WHEN I WAS IN GRADUATE SCHOOL back in the 1950s, D. H. Lawrence was considered one of the two great modern novelists writing in English, the other being James Joyce. The author of *Ulysses* was considered the great master of innovative language, structure, and narrative invention. But when it came to the complexity of human emotions, especially those involving subconscious sexual motivation, Lawrence was said to be the more "profound" of the two. In novels like *Sons and Lovers* (1913), *The Rainbow* (1915), and *Women in Love* (1920), Lawrence developed a new concept of fiction: human actions are determined not by psychological motives, whether overt or subconscious, but by somatic impulses of which the characters themselves are quite unaware. "You mustn't look in my novel for the old stable ego of the character," he wrote to his friend Edward Garnett in a famous and much parsed letter of 1914:

> There is another ego, according to whose action the individual is unrecognizable, and passes through, as it were, allotropic states which it needs a deeper sense than any we've been used to exercise to discover are states of the same single radically unchanged element. (Like as diamond and coal are the same pure single element of carbon. The ordinary novel would trace the history of the diamond — but I say, "diamond, what! This is carbon." And my diamond might be coal or soot, and my theme is carbon.)

Here "diamond" refers to the language of psychological motivation we find in the

Victorian novel, "carbon" to the unnameable sexual impulse at the core of being. In *Women in Love*, for example, Lawrence's imagery repeatedly undercuts a given character's actual thoughts. Thus, in the early scene in which Gerald Crich is sadistically "forcing [his] wheeling mare, which spun and swerved like a wind," to stand at the railroad crossing until the thunderous locomotive has gone by, Gudrun Brangwen finds herself horrified by Gerald's actions and yet "look[s] at him with black-dilated spell-bound eyes." Her attraction to Gerald cannot be verbalized or rationalized: it just is.

By the 1970s, Lawrence's reputation was in decline. His flirtation with Fascism in the early 1920s, his denigration of democracy and admiration for strong authoritarian leaders, and especially his purported misogyny and patriarchal politics came in for much rebuke in the wake of the feminist revolution: witness Kate Millett's *Sexual Politics* (1968), which argued that Lawrence's misunderstanding of female sexuality and "cult of the phallus" vitiated much of his fiction. In university courses in the United States, Lawrence's novels, once on every reading list, virtually disappeared from the canon. And the literary and cultural criticism, like the marvelously perceptive *Studies in Classic American Literature* (1923), with its satiric anatomy of Hawthorne's Puritanism and Lawrence's love-hate relationship with Whitman, came to be considered too eccentric.

The case of Lawrence the poet is a little different; never having attained the same heights as Lawrence the novelist or critic, he didn't have as far to fall. As early as 1935, R.P. Blackmur argued that Lawrence's poetry suffered from the "fallacy of expressive form": the belief that "if a thing is only intensely enough felt, its mere expression in words will give it satisfactory form." Blackmur was thinking primarily of Lawrence's love poems, and these did strike many later critics as merely diaristic. A handful of these poems — "Piano," "Song of a Man Who Has Come Through," "Snake," and "Bavarian Gentians" — have made their way into anthologies, but studies of modernist poetics have largely ignored Lawrence's poetry even though poets from Ezra Pound and William Carlos Williams to Robert Creeley, Allen Ginsberg, and Sylvia Plath have paid homage to it.

In the UK, Lawrence has never ceased being a major writer: the General Editor's Preface to the *Cambridge Edition of the Works of D.H. Lawrence* begins with a confident categorical statement that "D. H. Lawrence is one of the great writers of the twentieth century." The two volumes under review here (the 39th and 40th volumes of the Cambridge Edition) are to be complemented by yet a third volume, this one devoted entirely to unpublished poems. At that point, the Cambridge Edition will be complete. And what an edition it is! The complete poems, found in Volume 1 (along with the prefaces to the various volumes in which they originally appeared), are accompanied, in Volume 2, by a 120-page account of the composition, publication, and reception of all of Lawrence's individual poems and collections, followed by elaborate annotations for each and every poem, including variants and corrections, publication histories, and explanatory notes as well as cross-references. Christopher Pollnitz's editorial and textual practice in producing the two volumes could hardly be bettered: every Biblical, literary, mythological, and biographical reference and cross-reference is explained. Indeed, for anyone with a serious scholarly interest in Lawrence's poetry, the Cambridge Edition more than justifies its $250 price tag.

At the same time, I wonder whether this definitive edition — one unparalleled, I think, in the annals of Modernist poetry — will bring Lawrence the new readership he deserves. The earlier *Complete Poems*, edited by Vivian de Sola Pinto and F. Warren Roberts for Penguin (1994) runs to 1,700 pages and lists at $30; it, too, includes the various prefaces (though not in their different variants, as here) as well as a set (much more limited, of course) of textual and explanatory notes. So far as previously uncollected poems are concerned, the Cambridge Edition's main contribution is its inclusion of the 1916–19 sequences of curious little war poems under the titles "All of Us," "Bits," and "War Films," which have never before been published in book form. Pollnitz calls these poems "a valuable addition to the Lawrence canon" but to read the 13 pages that constitute this set of poetic exercises would seem to confirm the reservations of previous editors. A good portion of the "All of Us" lyrics are translations Lawrence made from a collection of Fellaheen songs put together by a German Egyptologist named Heinrich Schäfer under the title *Die Lieder eines ägyptischen Bauern*. "The Well in Africa," for example, reads as follows:

> Thou well of Kilossa, thy well-cords are of silver
> And a draught of thee is strength to a soul in hell.
> Kilossa, sweet well of my strength, thou corded with silk,
> Heal me, for in my soul I am not well.

Kilossa, the elaborate note tells us, is in Tanzania, where so many soldiers fighting under the British commander Jan Smuts lost their lives in a 1916 battle with the Germans. But Lawrence's little adaptation of Schäfer's text is hardly notable, and neither are such others as "The Wind, the Rascal" (also based on a Schäfer poem), even though this one was accepted by Harriet Monroe for *Poetry* in 1914:

> *(A girl, sitting alone at night, starts at the sound of the wind.)*
>
> The wind, the rascal, knocked at my door, and I said:

"My love is come."
But Oh, wind, what a knave thou art
Thus to make sport of a sorrowful heart!

Or again, consider "The Jewess and the V.C.," in which "a woman of [London's] East End," as the prostitute is designated in an earlier version, tells the young soldier who has been awarded a Victoria Cross:

Why, if you saw my limbs, how they shine on my body
What then would you do? Then for sure you would go
And die like a dog in a hole. 'Tis strange what a shoddy
Lover you make, such a hero in front of the foe.

This not only strikes a sour anti-Semitic note; its awkward rhymes ("body"/"shoddy") and contorted syntax (limbs "shin[ing] *on* my body") do little to make the supposedly ironic contrast — good in battle, bad in bed — interesting or moving. Indeed, the inclusion of such poems merely serves to remind us that when Lawrence is good, he is very, very good, but that when he is bad, he is horrid.

BUT ENOUGH OF THE HORRID. Even among Lawrence's earliest "Rhyming Poems," there is already a handful of the very, very good. Here is a short lyric called "Cherry Robbers" (1908):

Under the long dark boughs, like jewels red
In the hair of an Eastern girl
Hang strings of crimson cherries, as if had bled
Blood-drops beneath each curl.

Under the glistening cherries, with folded wings
Three dead birds lie:
Pale-breasted throstles and a blackbird, robberlings
Stained with red dye.

Against the hay-stack a girl stands laughing at me,
Cherries hung round her ears
Offers me her scarlet fruit: I will see
If she has any tears.

Here the quatrains, with their alternating five- and three-stress lines and simple rhymes ("girl"/"curl"; "me"/"see"; "ears"/"tears"), seem conventional enough, as does the opening metaphor in which cherries in the dark foliage are seen as jewels in the girl's dark ("Eastern") hair. But although this laughing girl, with "Cherries hung round her ears," offers the narrator "her scarlet fruit," this is hardly a ballad about a happy night of love under the cherry trees. For in lines 3–4, the "crimson" cherries are pictured as "blood-drops beneath each curl," and immediately the scene cuts to the "three dead birds [...] Stained with red dye" under the tree. Presumably these birds — the "pale-breasted throstles [song thrushes] and a blackbird" — were shot because they were "robberlings," destroying the cherry crop; in a subtle move, the poet identifies with their "robbery," even as the death image refers to the girl herself, whose "cherry" he has robbed. Like the cherry-picking scene in *Sons and Lovers*, which immediately precedes the first sexual encounter between Miriam and Paul — an encounter in which the virginal Miriam reluctantly agrees to offer her "scarlet fruit" to her demanding lover — "Cherry Robbers" links love-making to death. The concluding "I will see / If she has any tears" suggests that the lover wants his girl to weep — tears, after all, are a sign of life — even as he knows she is dead inside.

As even these early poems testify, Lawrence's particular poetic gift is his very special empathy for and identification with non-human life. The aesthetic distance of the Romantics — think of Keats's "Thou wast not born for death, immortal Bird!" in "Ode to a Nightingale" — gives way to a nervous, edgy lyric mode, whose point of view shifts easily between the human and non-human, but without sentimentalizing the latter. In "Love on the Farm," for example, the poem's protagonist, a young farmer's wife awaiting her husband's return in the evening, imagines him killing a rabbit for their dinner and identifies with it:

> The rabbit presses back her ears,
> Turns back her liquid, anguished eyes
> And crouches low, then with wild spring
> Spurts from the terror of his oncoming
> To be choked back, the wire ring
> Her frantic effort throttling:
>   Piteous brown ball of quivering fears!

The sight and smell of death is a form of sexual arousal. The husband now enters the room:

> With his hand he turns my face to him

> And caresses me with his fingers that still smell grim
> Of the rabbit's fur! God, I am caught in a snare!
> I know not what fine wire is round my throat
> I only know I let him finger there.

In the preface to *New Poems* (1918), Lawrence rejects the conventional verse form of these early rhyming poems, making the case for a poetry of "the immediate present," a present in which "there is no perfection, no consummation, nothing finished. The strands are all flying, quivering, intermingling into the web." The resultant free verse, an "instant poetry" that longs to be "the insurgent naked throb of the instant moment," makes its first appearance in *Look! We Have Come Through!* (1917). The sequence was conceived as a narrative with an "Argument" placed on the frontispiece:

> After much struggling and loss in love and in the world of man, the protagonist throws in his lot with a woman who is already married. Together they go into another country, she perforce leaving her children behind. The conflict of love and hate goes on between the man and the woman, and between these two and the world around them, till it reaches some sort of conclusion, they transcend into some condition of blessedness.

The reference is to Lawrence's elopement, in 1912, with Frieda von Richthofen Weekley, the German wife of an English professor of modern languages at Nottingham University, with whom Lawrence had briefly studied. Frieda, six years older than Lawrence, was bored with her marriage and had already had brief affairs with other men when Lawrence fell under her spell. For him, she represented the uninhibited sexuality he had not been able to find in "Miriam" (Jessie Chambers) or other girls. He also loved the idea that Frieda was a member (however minor) of the aristocracy, so unlike the bourgeoisie that the working-class Lawrence, whose father was a coal miner, never stopped resenting. The story of their tumultuous love affair has been told by countless witnesses, including Frieda herself in her rather melodramatic *Not I, But the Wind* (1934), which takes its title from the opening line of Lawrence's "Song of a Man who Has Come Through."

But despite the visionary rhetoric of this and neighboring poems, the reality was less glorious. No sooner had the lovers eloped to Germany than Frieda wanted to return to England to see her children, and she and Lawrence began to quarrel bitterly. The war years (1914–18) were a special nightmare: married to a German, Lawrence was subject to constant harassment by the British military authorities. So, for all the talk of the "blessedness" finally attained by the lovers, most of the poems in *Look! We Have Come Through!* deal openly — and sometimes tediously — with conflict, misery, and misunderstanding. "The night was a failure," begins "First Morning," "but why not — ?". "Fronleichnam" (the title is the name of a Bavarian village, though Lawrence perhaps chose it because *Leiche* is the German word for "corpse"), begins:

> You have come your way, I have come my way;
> You have stepped across your people, carelessly, hurting them all;
> I have stepped across my people, and hurt them in spite of our care.

And in "Mutilation" we read, "how it aches / Where she is cut off from me! / Perhaps she will go back to England."

No doubt it was such anguished personal poems that prompted Blackmur to object to the "fallacy of expressive form" in Lawrence's work. But there are superb poems here as well: consider imagist lyrics as "Green," with its conjunction of the "apple-green" dawn and the beloved's shining green eyes, or the ballad "River Roses,'" with its subtle contrast of "pale-green glacier water" and "simmering marsh," or "Gloire de Dijon," with its graphic treatment of a beloved's morning bath ritual. "Rabbit Snared in the Night," carries further the theme of "Love on the Farm," but this time the rabbit is no longer a symbol but itself the object of desire. And "Doe at Evening" concludes with these lines:

> Ah yes, being male, is not my head hard-balanced, antlered?
> Are not my haunches light?
> Has she not fled on the same wind with me?
> Does not my fear cover her fear?

One of the finest poems in the volume is "Bei Hennef," which begins,

> The little river twittering in the twilight
> The wan, wondering look of the pale sky,
>   This is almost bliss.

That "almost" is a Lawrentian signature: it signals the poet's ability to step back and look at himself from an external perspective, to get at the "carbon" of his inner self. After some more description of the peaceful twilight and the "soft 'Sh!' of the river/ That will last for ever," Lawrence launches into one of his abstract disquisitions: "You are the call, and I am the answer, / You are the wish, and I the fulfillment." But just when the reader wonders how much of this bombast — what Lawrence himself burlesqued, with reference to Walt Whitman's lapses, as "CHUFF! CHUFF! CHUFF!" — one can take, we get this:

> What else? it is perfect enough.
> It is perfectly complete,
> You and I,
> What more—?
>
> Strange, how we suffer in spite of this!

The final deflationary turn nicely punctures the balloon of the speaker's self-important rhetoric. Paradoxically, Lawrence's erotic poetry only succeeded when he could distance himself both from his obsession with Frieda and also from his latent attraction to young men, which began to manifest itself in the later war years. Indeed, it was only when Lawrence came to question the very possibility of the sexual fulfillment his "demon" had long idealized that he could write brilliant poems about erotic encounters with the non-human.

The title of what Lawrence himself considered his best book of poems, *Birds, Beasts and Flowers* (1923), comes from Sabine Baring-Gould's familiar "Child's Evening Hymn": "Now the darkness gathers, / Stars begin to peep, / Birds, and beasts and flowers / Soon will be asleep." The devotional connection is not coincidental: one of Lawrence's most delightful essays, "Hymns in a Man's Life' (1928), pays tribute to the "rather banal Noncomformist hymns that penetrated through and through my childhood." The word "Galilee," for example, "sent shivers down my spine": "To me the word Galilee has a wonderful sound. The Lake of Galilee! I don't want to know where it is. I never want to go to Palestine. Galilee is one of those lovely glamorous words, not places, that exist in the golden haze of a child's half-formed imagination."

In *Birds, Beasts and Flowers*, such wonder is experienced when the poet defamiliarizes everyday fruit and flowers, animals and insects. Take "Peach," which begins:

> Would you like to throw a stone at me?
> Here, take all that's left of my peach.
>
> Blood-red, deep;
> Heaven knows how it came to pass.
> Someone's pound of flesh rendered up.

Lawrence's free verse has often been compared to Whitman's, but there is, in fact, little that is Whitmanesque in these jagged, nervous, conversational lines, with their abrupt, disjointed phrasing and aggressive mode of address. In Italy, where he wrote these poems, Lawrence had been studying F. T. Marinetti's Futurist manifestos, and

"Peach" begins on a note of Marinettian buffoonery, its speaker a mock-victim challenging his interlocutor(s) to cast the first stone. The opening identification with Christ is quickly undermined, and we realize that a peach stone — a single seed encased in hard wood — is in fact large enough to throw at someone and cause pain. The peach is a conventional symbol of beauty and sensuousness, of Edenic pleasure: it functions as such in endless metaphors about young girls who are compared to peaches. But Lawrence is interested not in what peaches look like or what they symbolize but in what they *are*. Thus the imagery of lines 3–5 refers to the fact that the flesh of the round peach is very soft and delicate (like breasts? buttocks?) but also easily bruised and hence, like Shylock's mandated "pound of flesh," associated with pain. The character of "peachness" is now brilliantly rendered:

> Wrinkled with secrets
> And hard with the intention to keep them.
>
> Why, from silvery peach-bloom,
> From that shallow-silvery wine-glass on a short stem
> This rolling, dropping, heavy globule?
>
> I am thinking, of course, of the peach before I ate it.

In the West, the peach tree, native to China, has always had exotic connotations. But no sooner has the poet mentioned the silvery peach blossom, than he reminds himself that soon it will give way to the "rolling, dropping, heavy globule": the unattractive thick liquid drop of the ripe fruit when bitten into. When over-ripe, the peach's skin, like a vain lady's, is "wrinkled with secrets." "Wrinkled" suggests that the peach is soft and mushy to the touch, but this peach, after what seems like a sex change, is also "hard with the intention to keep" its secrets. Subverting the fruit's usual feminine connotations, Lawrence's peach is evidently bisexual. The series of rhetorical questions that follow has an absurdist edge:

> Why so velvety, why so voluptuous heavy?
> Why hanging with such inordinate weight?
> Why so indented?
> Why the groove?
> Why the lovely bivalve roundnesses?
> Why the ripple down the sphere?
> Why the suggestion of incision?

Here Lawrence takes the actual botanical attributes of the peach and turns its nature into a mystery: when you see it whole, with its velvety surface and thin groove down the center, it looks enchanting. But the incision spoils it all: "Why was not my peach round and finished like a billiard ball? / It would have been if man had made it." Perfection, Lawrence suggests, is itself unnatural, and hence suspect: it is precisely the "groove," the "incision," that differentiates the body of the peach from the "perfect" balls machines can make. But no one wants to hear this truth, and so, in a final ironic gesture, the poet proffers his auditor not the peach but the peach stone. This, he implies, half in jest, is all we deserve.

"Peach," "Pomegranate," "Fig": the voice that speaks in these poems is at once aggressive and bemused, belligerent and light-hearted. It is a voice less lyrical than theatrical and performative: the voice not of a man enslaved to the fallacy of expressive form but rather that of a master rhetorician. Alternately a rapt witness and a bemused skeptic, this Lawrence is overheard in dialogue with mosquitoes and tortoises, snakes and sorb-apples, trying to place himself in relation to all that is other in his world. "Whenever [Lawrence] forgets about men and women with proper names and describes the anonymous life of stones, waters, forests, animals, flowers," W. H. Auden remarked in his brilliant essay on Lawrence in *The Dyer's Hand*,

> [the poet] forgets about men and women with proper names and describes the anonymous life of stones, waters, forests, animals, flowers [...] his bad temper and his dogmatism immediately vanish and he becomes the most enchanting companion imaginable, tender, intelligent, funny and, above all, happy.

"Happy" may be an exaggeration — Lawrence, whatever the subject, is never happy for long — but the mercurial, playful language of the animal poems is certainly unique. One of the finest in *Birds, Beasts and Flowers* is the long poem "Fish," a witty, sardonic treatment of identity quite different from, say, Elizabeth Bishop's "The Fish," in which the line between subject and object is never crossed. Lawrence, for his part, addresses the fish directly:

> Your life a sluice of sensation along your sides,
> A flush at the flails of your fins, down the whorl of your tail,
> And water wetly on fire in the grates of your gills;
> Fixed water-eyes.

Sometimes he assumes the voice of the prophet:

> Who is it ejects his sperm in the naked flood?
> In the wave-mother?

> Who swims enwombed?

And, at the climax of the poem, he tries to *become* a fish:

> To have the element under one, like a lover;
> And to spring away with a curvetting click in the air,
> Provocative.
> Dropping back with a slap on the face of the flood,
> And merging oneself!
>
> To be a fish!

The poet knows it can't work. Suddenly, the meditation shifts ground, the narrator moving outside the frame and now referring to fish in the third-person plural ("Admitted, they swim in companies, / Fishes") and returning to his everyday self: "But sitting in a boat on the Zeller lake / And watching the fishes in the breathing waters / Live and swim and go their way — / I said to my heart, *who are these?*" Recognizing his difference from the fish, the speaker now defines himself as just another fish-killer:

> I have waited with a long rod
> And suddenly pulled a gold-and-greenish, lucent fish from below,
> And had him fly like a halo round my head,
> Lunging in the air on the line.
>
> Unhooking his gorping, water-horny mouth,
> And seen his horror-tilted eye

Lawrence does not moralize the situation. Having seen the fish from just about every angle, he steps back: "But I, I only wonder / And don't know."

Perhaps the most frightening of Lawrence's animal poems is "Bat," which begins on an everyday note with the poet sitting on the terrace of his Florence house, watching the sunset. As the sky darkens, a green light enters against-stream," and suddenly "you see things flying." What things? "Swallows with spools of dark thread sewing the shadows together." Or so it seems. Tracking the "parabola" flight of these "swallows," the narrator suddenly realizes they are something else: "A twitch, a twitter, an elastic shudder in flight, / And serrated wings against the sky / Like a glove, a black glove thrown up at the light / And falling back." By this point, the reader has adopted the speaker's position and shares his "uneasy creeping in one's scalp." It is the inability to make contact with these blind creatures that makes the observer so uneasy: these "Little lumps that fly in air and have voices indefinite, wildly vindictive; / Wings like bits of umbrella" cannot be mastered or domesticated:

> Hanging upside down like rows of disgusting old rags, to sleep;
> And grinning in their sleep.
> Bats!
>
> In China the bat is a symbol of happiness.
>
> Not for me!

The final petulant, almost comic note is vintage Lawrence: he admits he may be wrong but sometimes being wrong is a necessity. In its precision, concision, and careful rhythmic articulation, "Bat" seems to me an almost perfect poem.

AFTER *BIRDS, BEASTS AND FLOWERS*, Lawrence's poetry largely declined. In his last seven years — years of illness and trauma — he wrote the poems collected in *Pansies* (1929), *Nettles* (1930), and the posthumous *Last Poems* (1932). In the introduction to *Pansies*, Lawrence tells us that these poems are offered as

> a bunch of *pensées* [...] a handful of thoughts. Or if you will have the other derivation of pansy, from *panser*, to dress or soothe a wound [...] Each little piece is a thought; not a bare idea of an opinion or a didactic statement, but a true thought, which comes as much from the heart and the genitals as from the head.

But despite this disclaimer, the bulk of Lawrence's "pansies" are direct statements, opinionated and often shrill. They express all of the poet's pet peeves: his scorn of chastity on the one hand and "mental" sex on the other; his contempt for the middle class; his mistrust of democracy; and his passionate hatred of technology and urbanism.

Every now and then, however, the quirky brilliance of *Birds, Beasts and Flowers* returns. "The Sea, The Sea," for example, presents the death/rebirth cycle in terms of sugar/salt imagery:

> Once the moon comes down

and the sea gets hold of us
cities dissolve like rock-salt
and the sugar melts out of life
iron washes away like an old blood-stain
gold goes out into a green shadow
money makes even no sediment
and only the heart
glitters in salty triumph
over all it has known, that has gone now into salty nothingness.

Here sea salt is seen as a kind of "destroyer and preserver" (like Shelley's West Wind), having the power to dissolve the mineral world — even gold and silver, not to mention iron — and so the heart can "glitter in salty triumph / over all it has known, that has gone now." The adverb "now," in this complex pattern of assonance, is no longer a part of "k*now*n"; it reverses the *o-n* of "g*on*e" to yield "nothingness."

The Last Poems Notebook contains such well-known anthology pieces as "Bavarian Gentians" and "The Ship of Death": poems much more conventional than "Bats" or "Fish" in their acceptance of death as a form of release from the pain of life. At his best, however, Lawrence, who would die at 45 from tuberculosis, mocks the very possibility of "readiness / for the longest journey." This is the Lawrence who remains one of our great modernist ironists. We find him in "Bare Almond-Trees," a poem that inverts the biblical, koranic, and kabbalistic imagery of almond tree and almond blossom as well as the commonplaces in travel literature, extolling the beauties of the Sicilian village of Taormina, where the poem was written. The "black almond trunks, in the rain," seen from "beneath the [poet's] terrace rail," come to look "Like iron implements twisted, hideous," like "Steel [...] sensitive steel, curving thinly and brittly up in a parabola." In the third stanza, the trees become downright ominous, seeming to give off electric charges in their "steel tips [...] Like some strange magnetic apparatus." But this familiar Romantic rant against technology takes a curious turn in its final stanza:

Sicily, December's Sicily in a mass of rain
With iron branching blackly, rusted like old, twisted implements
And brandishing and stooping over earth's wintry fledge, climbing the slopes
Of uneatable soft green!

The irony of that last line is quintessentially, and brilliantly, Lawrentian. How seductively "soft," the poet notes, is the "green" of those mountain slopes beyond the iron railings. But don't be fooled. It is also, for us humans, "uneatable." ✦

GEZI PARKINDA BIR KUŞ YUVASI

MÜESSER YENIAY

Nâzım Hikmet'e saygıyla

Bir kuş yuvasından yazıyorum bunları
iki dal arasında, Gezi parkında
göğsüme bıçak gibi saplanıyor nefesim
göğü yıkmaya geliyorlar bütün yeryüzü halkıyla

bir kuş yuvasıyım Gezi parkında
iki dal arasında

burada insanlar zehirli
ağaçlar sökülmüş

kovuluyoruz annemizin
bizi davet ettiği dünyadan

kuş seslerini bombalıyorlar
- çıkaramaz kuşlar çil çil para sesini -

bir Ethem duyuluyor ateşler içinde Anka!
kaynak işçisi Ankara'da…
yığılıyor bedeni kuş tüyü gibi.

ölmeden toprak ediyorlar bizi
duman altında sokak çocukları ve kediler
kambur sırtlarında kaybolan rüya
kör gözlerle dünyaya bakılmaz artık...
ya uyumak hiç ummadığın bir anda!
hiç ummadığın anda uyumak...

ben bir kuş yuvasıyım Gezi parkında
bir çift dal arasında

THE BIRD NEST IN GEZI PARK

For Nâzım Hikmet

I am writing these from a bird nest
between two branches in Gezi Park
like a knife my breath is stuck in my chest
they are coming to destroy the sky with all the people of earth

I am a bird nest in Gezi Park
between two branches

here the people are poisonous
the trees are uprooted

we are getting dismissed from
where our mothers invited us

they are bombing the twitters of birds
- birds cannot produce the sound of cash -

an Ethem is heard, a simurg in fire!
welding worker in Ankara
his body is collapsing like a feather

they are making us earth before dying
under smoke street children and cats …
on their hunchback a lost dream
with blind eyes cannot be looked at the world...
or to sleep in an unexpected moment!
in an unexpected moment to sleep...

I am a bird nest in Gezi Park
between a pair of branches

HARRIS

Unspoiled Monster: On Truman Capote

ROBERT PRANZATELLI

- 1 -

ONE SPRING IN THE LATE 1980S I sat at a large wooden table in the New York Public Library, in a room dedicated to rare holdings, and looked through a number of Truman Capote's holograph manuscripts, notebooks, and typed drafts. I had gained admission through tact and a bookish appearance, with no scholarly credentials, to see for myself what tidbits of the late author's unpublished work might await discovery. There weren't many, but to handle the pages on which my favorite writer had written his sentences gave me a new and subtle satisfaction.

One pearl I did find was an abandoned fragment, a sort of prose poem about Eastern Long Island, where Capote had lived for the last 20 years of his life. In two lovely paragraphs he stated his preference for

> that moment when the light goes yellow, that late October moving to November moment when the light of ocean-salted afternoons coldly burns like the drifting gold of dying leaves. Then overhead wild geese! — herds honking southward in loosely waving lines. Wild geese and wild duck; and wild swans undulating on the darkening ponds that flicker among the potato fields.

With characteristic vitality and grace, Capote evokes the milieu he has chosen to describe, in sentences that merge lyricism, drama, and sharp observation:

> A small red fox is seen at dusk stalking the lonely sea-edged sand-moors. Owls, residing in scrub-pine thickets, warn pheasants of creeping human hunters [...]

In another fragment — the opening paragraphs of an unfinished magazine piece, probably begun in the last year or so of his life — I encountered a different season and setting, and a variation of his narrative voice:

> Snowflakes large as leaves lingered in the air. I was happy to rid myself of a cold Park Avenue, exchange it for the warmth of the Waldorf Towers. I was happy anyway. I always was when I was going to spend an evening with Cole Porter.

Here is the author as socialite, awaited by his host in the famous songwriter's "dazzling" library, where, amid tortoise-shell walls, "the book-shelves, strewn with books and bowls of white lilac, were bars of golden brass."

As I sat among his stray beguiling sentences I felt sad about the pages he didn't write, the works he couldn't finish, but also more deeply aware of the magnitude of what he had completed — and I believed with great certainty that time would only strengthen the recognition of Capote's literary accomplishments. In a sense, I was right. In the decade and a half that followed, most of his published works remained in print, widely available in bookstores; those few that slipped out of print didn't usually do so for long, and were easily obtainable in public libraries. Then, the years 2004 through 2007 brought a windfall: the release of two major films based on Capote's life, three significant anthologies (devoted, respectively, to his stories, letters, and essays), several reissues of other books by or about him — and, like a miraculous gift from the blue, the discovery and publication of Capote's long-lost apprentice novella *Summer Crossing*. And, spurred on by the success of the 2005 film *Capote*, the paperback edition of *In Cold Blood* returned to the bestseller lists, where it lodged near the top for several months.

But I was wrong about one thing. In my wide-eyed idealism I had believed that the sensationalistic glow of Capote's personal problems would inevitably fade, along with any other shallow forms of notoriety, to be eclipsed by a growing public awareness of his greatness as an artist. That leap of faith has proven very naïve indeed; still, I retain a certain thin strand of idealism, enough to sustain my belief that the indisputably brilliant young man displayed in "The Exuberant Years," the aptly titled first section of *Too Brief a Treat: The Letters of Truman Capote* (2004), and the complicated middle-aged man he later became, will be remembered for the right reasons: not the oft-repeated litany of addictions to fame, drugs, and alcohol, but the more meaningful addictions to language, memory, mood, and narrative. I like to revisit him where he was at his best, on the page, and to recall with affection the artful raconteur.

- 2 -

CAPOTE WAS THE PROSE POET OF AMERICAN SELF-CREATION, the theme of inventing or re-inventing oneself. His first book, *Other Voices, Other Rooms* (1948), a bizarre coming-of-age novel, cloaks its homosexual theme in a lush jungle of poetic language; in this almost hallucinogenic Southern psychodrama, it's nearly impossible to distinguish between coming out, staying in, and drowning in an exquisite sea of Freudian-Gothic literary styling. But while the ambiguity may derive from the social constraints of the late 1940s, when the book was composed and published, the indirection enhances the artistry: submerged in the fantastic, the story's psychosexual tension fascinates.

Although it can be seen as setting the bright "day" world of childhood, innocence, natural beauty, and consciousness against a dark "night" world of adulthood, corruption, the grotesque, and the subconscious, the novel is done an injustice by such a reductive interpretation. In the world of *Other Voices* the children are as quirky, as driven, as full of strange mysteries, as the adults; Idabel and Florabel, the sisters Joel befriends, are as extreme, in their own way, as most of the other characters. Nobody, young or old, is thoroughly innocent (Idabel is violent and intimidating, Florabel is self-centered and manipulative, and Joel harbors a wide range of conflicting thoughts and impulses); the natural world, even at its sunniest and most pleasant, is described in language that lends a sense of strangeness and wild instability; and because of the intensity with which the story is told, the entire book, including the sections dealing with comparatively ordinary events, seems set in a landscape of the unconscious. Rather than two types of reality pitted against each other, there is one very intimidating otherworldly place — a place of mystery, wonder, loss, desire, sin, empathy, tragedy, and consolation — in which the narrator is trapped and to which he must adapt. Joel can only achieve that adaptation by defining himself, as a man, as a sexual being, and as the center of power in his own life.

Similarly, in *Breakfast at Tiffany's* (1958), Holly Golightly's moral ambiguity, far from being worrisome, is presented as one more reason to love her: she, like all of us, is a chameleon struggling to find the right color. A self-invented creature, Holly Golightly is not her real name, and she has designed her presentation of herself to create a glamorous aura and elicit the all-important blessings of social acceptance. Capote portrays her as no mere phony but as a kind of artist, an artist of social movement, like himself. An obvious fantasy-double of the author, Holly possesses the nerve to transcend her humble rural origins and the station to which she was born, and embodies the Capote drive to make life livelier and more artful.

Beneath the need to change and climb lie desperate motives and intense anxiety. The stakes are high; those individuals who do not somehow invent or exceed themselves are left to sink into mediocrity, like the more ignorant townspeople of *The Grass Harp* (1951) — the sheriff, Big Eddie Stover, the minister, and his wife — or the superficially beautiful but essentially destructive jetsetters in the unfinished *Answered Prayers* (1986). More frightening still, life may shape them into psychotic monsters, like the murderers in *In Cold Blood* (1965). At the very beginning of his career, in macabre stories such as "Miriam" and "The Headless Hawk," Capote explored a kind of inversion of self-creation, the fates of characters haunted by what might be disowned aspects of themselves, in the form of eerie presences and doppelgängers. His adept use of the "double" — grotesque, comic, enigmatic — demonstrated precocious mastery of an age-old theme that had fascinated Poe and would fascinate Nabokov; and his sly use of the "devil's bargain" theme in "Children on Their Birthdays" struck yet another mischievously dark-humored cautionary note regarding misguided personal aspiration.

Capote's trilogy of autobiographical tales "A Christmas Memory," "The Thanksgiving Visitor," and "One Christmas" portrays the reverse of his usual equation: Miss Sook Faulk, an elderly eccentric incapable of being anything other than her gentle generous self, represents the antithesis of personal reinvention and is clearly the saintly role model, while the author-narrator's divorced parents, who make separate appearances in "One Christmas," are each destructively self-centered; in their desperate grasping at the social ladder, they abandon their child. That child remains helpless to do anything but love them, even as their behavior destroys his self-esteem. Here the author reveals the wellspring of his need to recreate himself, which in turn explains his affinity for others (fictional or real) who share this painful drive and, like him, turn it, for a while at least, into an artistic gift. But in his reverence for Miss Sook, who throughout all three stories stands for morality and compassion, he acknowledges that her kind of person — stable, without pretense, unchanging in her sense of decency — is the bedrock on which healthier lives are built.

The theme of aspiration toward a newer, greater, more impressive, or more liberated identity runs throughout the history of literature, and features prominently in the literature of 20th-century America — perhaps because America has been an ongoing experiment in social and spiritual redefinition. Whether it is Fitzgerald's Gatsby, Salinger's Glass family, or Celie in Alice Walker's *The Color Purple* — to cite just a few popular examples — many characters in American literature are the instruments of their own redefinition. They try to transform their identities through means that may be economic (Gatsby) or philosophical (the Glasses), or through the discovery of links between spirituality, self-esteem, and human rights

(Celie). In response to the social forces that seek to shape them, they instead reshape themselves, in an effort to elude limitations and oppression, and, in most cases, to turn the tables on the prevalent social order, forcing it to shift and make room.

Capote's protagonists, however, are largely apolitical and unconcerned with changing the social order: most either want to climb it or be lovingly consoled. Or, perhaps, both: the theatrical performers in *The Muses Are Heard* (1956) want, like all performers, to garner rave reviews and audience approval, to score a social coup and win heaps of demonstrative love — a collection of goals Capote satirized but shared.

- 3 -

IN HIS WIDELY HAILED "nonfiction novel" *In Cold Blood*, Capote's lyrical and gossipy impulses are subsumed within a tone of studied objectivity and grim irony. Regarded by many as both the centerpiece and apex of Capote's career, the book's deftly orchestrated suspense narrative makes it riveting on first reading — and its unflinching account of human brutality makes it difficult to reread, despite the classical beauty of its composition. Returning to its prose for a slower, more careful examination after the plot's page-turning qualities have subsided, however, one discovers Capote's well-practiced penchants for lyricism, hyperbole, and satiric description, alongside the stoically delivered ironies and the litanies of sometimes grim detail. One of the murderers has a face "which seemed composed of mismatching parts. It was as though his head had been halved like an apple, then put together a fraction off center" — a creepy portrait that could as easily emanate from a macabre tale in *A Tree of Night and Other Stories* (1949). Many of the Holcomb townspeople resemble the denizens of a Capote comedy, introduced with characteristic brio: the local mail messenger, known as Mother Truitt, a rather youthful 75-year-old, is a "stocky, weathered widow who wears babushka bandannas and cowboy boots." The local postmistress, Mrs. Clare, is

> a gaunt, trouser-wearing, woolen-shirted, cowboy-booted, ginger-colored, gingery-tempered woman of unrevealed age ("That's for me to know, and you to guess") but promptly revealed opinions, most of which are announced in a voice of rooster-crow altitude and penetration.

In audio recordings of Capote reading passages from his writings, the notoriously odd-voiced author exhibits hilarious comic timing and a brilliant flair for performance with a passage from *Breakfast at Tiffany's*, and he mixes, without hesitation, comic flourishes into his readings of certain passages from *In Cold Blood*, as well. One realizes that Capote's mischievous impulses were not abandoned for the latter, only redeployed into a smaller supporting role; held in check but used as a counterpoint that serves to heighten, through contrast, the tragic vision that informs the book. In the decade and a half that followed — in *Answered Prayers*, an acid portrait of high society, and in the collection *Music for Chameleons* (1980) — Capote's prose would become leaner and sleeker, but less decorous: as the years passed, he wrote with more sheer nerve than ever before.

Answered Prayers is a fictionalized spilling of vicious gossip accumulated through decades of social climbing and scandalmongering. Sexual curiosities, ribald anecdotes, and social and literary in-jokes pile up in a never-resolved storyline darting back and forth through time and across continents, with flashbacks within flashbacks, stories within stories within stories, and a crowd of colorful characters, disguised and undisguised, fictional and real. The most infamous chapter, "La Côte Basque," a brilliantly rendered set piece, is best read as a separate long story, one of Capote's finest, rather than as an incongruous part of an unfinished novel. Although originally intended to be fitted in as one of the book's later chapters, it was in fact written (and published in *Esquire* magazine) prior to the novella-length opening chapter "Unspoiled Monsters" and its successor "Kate McCloud"; all three pieces share the same first-person narrator, but "La Côte Basque" is much closer in tone to the carefully controlled third-person short story "Mojave" that preceded it, and it shares almost nothing of the other two chapters' elaborate plotlines and characters. (Capote's biographer Gerald Clarke has written that he believes Capote would have eventually removed "La Côte Basque" from the novel, and in fact its first appearance in a book, presumably with its author's approval, was as a self-contained story in the 1983 anthology *Great Esquire Fiction*. I wish it had also been included in the 2004 collection *The Complete Stories of Truman Capote*, where, as one of Capote's only later fictional works, it would have been a hugely important addition.)

"Unspoiled Monsters" and "Kate McCloud" share a quite different tone and fit together; they can be read as a separate work written in an over-the-top prose style — hyperbolic, hypnotic, and embroidered with alliteration, bitchiness, and lewd language. There is a hint of a literary crisis to come: the narrator, an unlucky writer at work on a book to be called *Answered Prayers*, admits that he never manages to finish anything.

Beneath the hard exterior of both the character and the story, flashes of humanity can be glimpsed, as when the narrator dreams of redemption through an act of heroism or finds himself defending Times Square degenerates from the verbal harassment of a self-righteous street preacher. The immorality celebrated in the novel's gossip seems a setup for an arrival of enlightenment intended for a later chapter, never delivered. Capote once said that the reader would close the book with a smile and a tear, that the book was "one of the few novels I know that has a genuinely happy ending."

Is *Answered Prayers* a Zen riddle disguised as a dirty joke? In its unfinished state it resembles a koan, an unanswerable question or unresolvable paradox designed to provoke thought. That this Prayer is unanswerable leaves the reader free to trace imaginary lines, navigate the odd narrative construction and swift word-currents, play with a few jigsaw puzzle pieces, and test the combinations, attempting with tantalizing mounds of evidence to second-guess an inspired artist — which of course is impossible.

Yet there are clues: "I finished 'Mojave' late last night — and the one thing I do know: all these people are the same person and their stories are the same story, one inserted into the other, like Russian nesting dolls. In fact, I think that image may well apply to everything described in these pages." These were the opening two sentences of the chapter entitled "Kate McCloud" as it originally ran in magazine form; for book publication, they were cut, along with all references to the story "Mojave" (which Capote removed from *Answered Prayers* and included instead in *Music for Chameleons*). The magazine version reflects the author's original plan to present "Mojave" as a story composed by P. B. Jones, the narrator. It would have been another of the novel's many stories-within-stories and by far the longest — too distracting a diversion. The Russian nesting doll metaphor, however, aptly describes the book's structure and its author's concept of the contrivance he wished to craft. It may also describe his view of the human personality: identities hidden within identities.

If all the stories are the same story, they are all, on at least a symbolic level, Capote's story, an ascent and descent through a world where personal reinvention and social triumph mix with corruption and desperation, as seen by the embittered, wounded adult who had once been, and in some ways still was, the little boy who loved Cousin Sook of "A Christmas Memory" — the man with a dual vision: a vision of amorality (worn as an armor of self-preservation) and sentimentality (buried far beneath the malicious gossip, but ready to soar up at the end of the novel).

The core of *Answered Prayers*, however, is not psychology but aesthetics: Capote aimed to create a tour de force of wit, style, and perfectly sculpted prose. In an interview near the end of his life, he said of Flaubert, a strong influence, "He was more concerned with style than content. Content with him was like he would take an apple out of a basket and put it on a table and say, 'Now I'm going to do this apple.' I mean, I don't think he really gave a fuck about *Madame Bovary*. He cared how it all shaped itself, how real he could make it." What mattered to Flaubert's disciple, Capote, were sentences, shades, how a subject could be stylized to maximum effect — the reshaping of the identities of people and the reshaping of their stories.

- 4 -

THE APTLY TITLED *MUSIC FOR CHAMELEONS* BRIMS WITH CHARACTERS that are, or want to be, changelings of one kind or another. In "Mr. Jones" a crippled old man turns out to be something other than what he pretends; in "A Lamp in a Window" an apparently ordinary spinster reveals a secret that transforms the reader's perception of her; in "Mojave" numerous characters engage in carefully orchestrated infidelities, their slippery loyalties illustrating how even those we think we know best possess the disturbing human capacity for shifting identity. In "Dazzle" the autobiographical narrator recounts the tale of his boyhood aspiration to be magically transformed into a girl. In "Then It All Came Down" and the novella-length "Handcarved Coffins," Capote comes face-to-face with two of the most frightening chameleons of all, homicidal minds capable of multiple murders. In "A Day's Work" he accompanies a cleaning lady on her rounds and spies, hilariously and touchingly, on the secret selves her clients hide from the outside world. In the Marilyn Monroe profile "A Beautiful Child" he elevates an afternoon of gossipy conversation into an indirect meditation on the transformative and corrosive powers of celebrity and insecurity, and in a final self-interview ("Nocturnal Turnings, or How Siamese Twins Have Sex") he splits himself into two halves to analyze his own complex and ever-changing self — his final variation on the theme of the double. Although often judged as a collection of separate pieces (and it can certainly be enjoyed that way — and critiqued that way, for its contents vary in quality), the book is also a carefully sequenced unit, its components echoing and balancing one another, its sculpted sentences and intricate implications summing up its author's four-decade career.

Capote's lyrical turns are not merely ornamental. In the mostly comic "A Day's Work," after a particularly comedic scene we encounter this striking sentence: "The rain had returned and the wind increased, a mixture that made the air look like a shattering mirror." Within the course of the next few paragraphs, Capote stands on Park Avenue alongside his cleaning lady (they are both stoned) and tells her (with "the downpour drenching us") of his mother's suicide. He does not explicitly connect the suicide to the foreshadowing image of rain and wind as "shattering mirror," but the reader feels, consciously or not, the connection, all the more powerful for the restraint with which it has been implied.

In the self-interview that concludes the book, Capote returns to a belief in God in the midst of depression and summons again the image of Sook, the one pillar of loving stability in his childhood and the closest thing to a lifeline he ever had. After a lifetime of trying to metamorphose into something other than the child he was, and a lifetime writing of characters, fictional and real, reaping the mostly bitter fruit of their mostly misguided struggles to transform themselves, he seems to embrace more than ever that which Sook represents: the ultimate wholeness of the guileless soul.

As interesting as this final piece is — and it rivals Wilde's *De Profundis* in its mix of egocentricity, artfulness, and insight — it's not as brilliant as the book's title piece, "Music for Chameleons." Here, in a handful of well-polished pages, readers are given what appears at first to be merely an exquisitely described afternoon visit with an elegant aristocrat in Martinique, not so much a story or essay as a bauble, a piece of prose jewelry.

"The most *subtle* story," Capote told Edmund White, "is 'Music for Chameleons.' Even sophisticated readers don't understand it. They think it's about a visit with a woman; they think it's a *travel* piece about Martinique. But it's actually a meditation on murder, about how our passions flog us."

The tension Capote sets up between the social graces passing between himself and his hostess, the unexpressed thoughts that he shares only with the reader, the subjects of conversation (ghosts, capital punishment, dangerous-looking masked figures at a street festival, the murder of a homosexual friend by two sailors he had met in a bar), and the eerie effects of a black mirror into which the author-narrator periodically gazes, turn this unique, understated piece of writing into a brilliant short story. Beneath the glaze of surface beauty it simmers with unsettling implications and poetic ambiguity; it sets the tone, and sets up the themes, of the entire volume, while providing the ideal title. ("Chameleons" can refer to the characters in this story, the characters in all the stories, the readers of the book — or all of the above.) The story's final image, of a piano played as chameleons scurry across a terrace in Martinique, is perfection: the music of Capote's prose attracts his chameleon readers with similar elegance. One thinks of Keats: "What shocks the virtuous philosopher delights the chameleon poet."

It is this nearly absurd insistence on art first — the unfailingly graceful rhythms of his sentences, the precision of his poetic description, the economy (to the point of phenomenal concision) of these miniatures — combined with his insistence on the populist virtue of never boring his audience — that makes Capote's best work so potent. His remarkable shrewdness can't fully mask the shortcomings of his intellect — he was not, and never aspired to be, an intellectual heavyweight — but his savvy in narrative construction, twinned with his incisive observations of characters and settings, allow him, like F. Scott Fitzgerald and J. D. Salinger, to build up even the flimsiest material with an exuberance so irresistible (an exuberance of language, of style, of the artist's sheer delight in playing the mischievous games of storytelling) that readers glow with the contagious pleasure of the prose. Rather than the synthesis and analysis of complex ideas and the marshaling of a wide range of knowledge to reinforce a new perception, he offers the distillation of experience into finely honed expression, and the marshaling of aesthetic effects to elicit a new sensibility — a different, but equally valid, equally valuable, form of prose art.

Given the degree to which Capote fictionalized it, I tend not to regard much of his supposedly nonfiction work as journalism. He did himself a disservice claiming it as such, and that disservice continues to affect the perception of his work. Readers of the handsome 2007 anthology *Portraits and Observations: The Essays of Truman Capote* (more than a third of which consists of pieces from *Music for Chameleons*) will likely scoff at the credibility gap whenever Capote drops a tall tale into the trappings of reportage; still, it's a marvelous collection, even if some of the pieces defy categorization, as "essays" or anything else.

Christopher Lehmann-Haupt struck a resonant note in his original *New York Times* review of *Music for Chameleons* in 1980, when he observed that Capote had "succeeded in projecting all the facets of his remarkable and varied personality" — including "the side of himself that delights in making up whoppers." I agree, and I would add that *Music for Chameleons* reports on the real world in much the way fine fiction does: provisionally, indirectly, subjectively, and, at times, hardly at all. Magicians are only interested in truth insofar as they can toy with it. Capote's great achievement was the summoning of the incantatory power of language, the deletion of anything that might impede the sensual rhythmic flow of his narratives, and the application of his skills to a widely varied selection of material. Drawn to subjects ranging from the sensational (and sensationalized) to the understated, he used his subject matter as a model with which to display his ability to stylize. ("Now I'm going to do this apple." Flaubert or Capote?) Yet the stylizing leads to a vision that illuminates the subjects chosen. Style and content become inseparable.

- 5 -

IN THE 1967 ESSAY "Ghosts In Sunlight," Capote states: "Reflected reality is the essence of reality, the truer truth [...] All art is composed of selected detail, either imaginary or, as in *In Cold Blood*, a distillation of reality." In the preface to his 1973 collection *The Dogs Bark*, he adds that "art is not distilled water: personal perceptions, prejudices, one's sense of selectivity pollute the purity of germless truth." These references to "distillation" and "selectivity" are about as close to an aesthetic theory as he got. An essay from 1955, "Style: and the Japanese," pays tribute to the way that, "like visual musicians, the Japanese seem to have perfect pitch in areas of shape and color." This very brief essay consists of only four long paragraphs; its heart is its opening, an affectionate childhood recollection of an elderly Japanese florist in New Orleans, who created for his young friend "a score of toys" — all handmade, elaborate, fantastical. They were "much too exquisite to be played with" but became the author's "original aesthetic experience — they made a world and set a standard of taste." The image of Mr. Mariko, the florist, selecting his materials and making "a world" ("one could never decide, watching him work at his arrangements, what made him choose between those brown leaves and that green vine so sophisticated, so accurate an effect") takes the reader to the center of the writer's identity. Mystery, precision, and a sense of setting standards of taste are all intertwined with the selectivity, the distillation, that makes a visual or verbal composition and creates the sensibility, new or refined, that is the artist's gift to his audience.

The pleasures of sensuality celebrated in Capote's writing sometimes intensify into a moment of transcendence; from sybarite to mystic suddenly seems a short jump. To experience a "moment of being" that combines profound awareness of natural beauty, an inexplicable sense of impending joy, and a sense of the miraculous in the midst of quiet, one can meditate in a monastery, seek guidance from a guru, or study Japanese scrolls — or simply linger over the following sentences from the 1967 essay "Extreme Magic":

> Now, leaving the warm moist southern climate, we steam steadily northward into spheres where the air, though it is only late August, trembles already with a

> beyond-September chill. It is as if a cold crystal ball had descended, enclosing and stilling the green sea, sky, the growing-greener coast bobbing by: gone is the harsh and stony Montenegrin grayness, the subtropic pallor, for now each northward-going day the scene is more fruitful, there are trees and fields of wild flowers and grape vineyards and shepherds munching close to the Adriatic's edge.
>
> I feel touched by some extreme magic, an expectant happiness — as I always do when that sense of autumn arrives, for autumn never seems to me an end but a start, the true beginning of all our new years.

Here, in three long sentences from what many critics would term a "minor travel sketch," we are transported, offered a moment not of religious revelation but of the tranquil beauty on which human spirituality and faith are built. Not surprisingly, this moving passage occurs near the end of a fashionable account of yachting with the conspicuously wealthy.

- 6 -

WHEN TRUMAN CAPOTE DIED in August 1984, one month short of his 60th birthday, I was 20. The world, I felt, had lost a genius, an extraordinarily sensitive writer. Despite the obvious "queerness" of his often-ridiculed public persona (or perhaps partly because of this — because he was an outsider) I had revered him as a kind of hero. Mostly, though, I found his heroism in his art. For me his work had set a standard of what prose could achieve, while his determination to master many forms of writing (stories, novels, travel sketches, reportage, scripts and screenplays, portraits, memoirs) inspired me as a young writer trying to acquire as many skills as possible.

Two and a half years after his death, on a freezing cold Sunday morning in late January 1987, I attended a lecture, part of a series called "Biographers and Brunch" at the 92nd Street Y Poetry Center in New York. The speaker, Gerald Clarke, had written but not yet published *Capote: A Biography*. (When it appeared, in 1988, it became a bestseller, and will likely remain the definitive work on its subject's life: a well-written, balanced portrait revealing Capote's strengths and flaws.) Mr. Clarke discussed writing the biography, regaled us with a few charming anecdotes, read from his work, and spoke of the headaches involved in sorting fact from fiction in the many accounts of the garrulous but ever-embellishing author's life. To illustrate Capote's tendency to twist the truth into a good tale, Clarke read a late-1950s piece on the meeting with Cocteau and Gide, then explained that after much digging he'd learned that Gide wasn't in the same country as Capote and Cocteau at the time Capote's account purports that the three met. Clarke, however, was amused, not scornful, in reporting this tendency to lie.

Mr. Clarke took a careful, hesitant approach to the audience's questions. I particularly recall those of a persistent elderly woman who insisted he should have told us more about Truman's tragic side. "More tragedy," she harped. "Would you tell us now a little about how tortured he was?"

He didn't, really, and neither have I. With rare lapses, Capote refused to play victim, preferring the more powerful roles of sinner, celebrant, and genius. More importantly, he left a body of work that turns every subject it embraces, however dark or light, into a vehicle for literary art, an aesthete's exquisitely crafted offering to any that choose to appreciate it. By doing so, he invented his most lasting self, the one that, as with all great writers, eclipses the mortal self that birthed it and radiates its own self-defined reality. We are left to accept this final, still mercurial, identity: a chameleon poet of shocks and delights. ✦

Rest in Peace: World War I and Living Memory

ELIAH BURES

[S]omething, or an infinite number of things, die in each death...
There was a day in time when the last eyes to see Christ
were closed forever. The battle of Junín and the love of Helen
died with the death of some one man.

Jorge Luis Borges
"The Witness"

The last survivor of World War I died on May 5, 2011, nearly 97 years after the war's outbreak in July 1914. This was Claude Stanley Choules, a veteran of the British Navy who had witnessed the surrender of the German High Seas Fleet in November 1918. The experience of trench warfare had already slipped from living memory two years earlier with the death of "the last fighting Tommy," Harry Patch, in July 2009. The course of 2008 saw the deaths of the last known Italian, Ukrainian, Polish, Hungarian, French, German, and Turkish veterans. The final survivors from Serbia and Belgium died in 2004, the last from Thailand and New Zealand in 2003, the last from Guyana in 2000, and the last Algerian in 1998. The last to serve in the Great War in any capacity was Florence Green, a mess steward in the British Women's Royal Air Force in the conflict's final months. Ms. Green passed away on February 4, 2012, a few weeks shy of her 111th birthday.

There is now no one alive who remembers the First World War at first hand. The memory of the Great War, like the memory of all wars, has been a powerful source of identity for those that fought it. But the personal witness of the war's estimated 65 million combatants has also done far more, shaping broader beliefs about the truth of warfare in the modern age. If World War II remains, to many, the "good war," its predecessor is the quintessential "pointless war," a cautionary tale of futile sacrifice and senseless industrialized slaughter, of militarism and nationalism run amok, and

of an arrogant civilization engineering its own decline. As one prominent veteran, the novelist Erich Maria Remarque, put it, the war was "a meaningless surface of things joined to an abyss of sorrow."

Today, with the Great War's passage from living memory behind us and its centenary just around the bend, the time has come to rethink the conflict's status as a poster child for the futility of war, a notion that has grown so myth-laden, so one-dimensional, so caricatured, that it does disservice to the anti-war agenda it was originally meant to advance. Indeed, those concerned with preventing war in the present may stand to benefit most from jettisoning this simplistic view of war in the past. A lack of realism, after all, has never been the best means of guarding against wickedness in the real world. In the midst of wolves, the Gospel tells us, we are to be wise as serpents.

Understanding how World War I became the "pointless war" requires understanding how the meanings assigned to the conflict have always been bound up with the witness of common soldiers. Coming on the heels of a 19th-century surge in literacy, World War I loosed an unprecedented flood of written retrospection. By no means all of these thousands of memoirs, diaries, and novels support a verdict of futility and meaninglessness. If some writers damned the conflict and the societies that waged

JACQUES MARLOW (IMAGE SOURCE: WIKIMEDIA COMMONS)

it, other accounts, often better selling at the time, purveyed a range of patriotic, idealistic, or redemptive interpretations. But it is the "anti-war myth" that has come to dominate our memory of the Great War, a view repeatedly endorsed in recent years by the dwindling ranks of World War I veterans. Appreciating not only what is lost with the loss of living memory but what is gained as well can help us draw new lessons from the war George Kennan rightly called the "great seminal catastrophe" of the 20th century.

CLAIMS FOR THE VALUE OF LIVING MEMORY ARE OF TWO GENERAL KINDS. The first concerns the vividness and accessibility of the past. "It is as though once living memory has been lost," the literary critic Christopher Clausen suggested, "the event itself — its mixture of valor and horror, its power to warm or inspire, its sheer reality — becomes irrevocably diminished." Reflecting on his conversations with American veterans of the Great War, the writer David Laskin argued that what we are deprived of is "more akin to poetry than history — an impression of the past... more textured, emotionally complex, and, in some ways, more baffling than anything [to be] gleaned from books, diaries, letters, photos, or film clips." As one journalistic commentator on the passing of the World War I generation put it, their deaths "relegate the cataclysm they saw with their own eyes to the bloodless abstraction of recorded history."

A second, related claim is a variation on the old adage that those who fail to remember the past are condemned to repeat it. We invest the memory of calamitous events like war and genocide with a kind of moral force. The firsthand witness becomes the authoritative bearer, not only of a tale to be told (what it was like), but a lesson to be learned (what it meant). Like its legal counterpart, the moral witness offers to ensure some measure of future justice: if not "never again," then at least "never forget."

But the loss of living memory can also bring with it a liberation from entanglement in the past, and from the distortions to which all memory — individual or collective — is inevitably prone. The stories of eyewitnesses, sometimes even their sheer presence, can cast a powerful spell over the minds of contemporaries. It is hardly coincidental, Claussen noted, that the American South's resistance to desegregation began to diminish around the same time that those southerners who had grown up with Confederate veterans seated around the Sunday dinner table left the political scene.

Might the Great War generation's passing offer a similar liberation from the sway of living memory? Popular awareness of the war today, it should be noted, varies strikingly by national context. For most of Central and Eastern Europe, the events of 1914-1918, though no less bloody than elsewhere, have long since been overshadowed by subsequent invasions, revolutions, and civil wars. Fought by empires which were consumed by the war itself, and which often mobilized subject minorities against their own peoples (some two million Poles, for instance, were scattered throughout the German, Russian, and Austro-Hungarian armies), the First World War was a conflict of old elites and ancient dynasties. For countries like Poland and Russia, the war's conclusion did not so much end armed conflict as inaugurate a wave of territorial disputes and political struggles. Poland, which fought Russians, Lithuanians, Ukrainians, and Belorussians on its eastern border, was not at peace until 1921. Extending and consolidating their 1917 seizure of power cost the Bolsheviks six more years of conflict. The fighting most formative for later collective identities, in other words, took place not during the war, but afterward.

For those nations that fought on the Western Front, World War I has found a more lasting place in the popular imagination. This is less true of the United States, which, though it sustained more combat deaths (approximately 53,000) in the few months of its effective involvement in the war than in the two decades of its presence in Vietnam, pays scant attention to the conflict. Snoopy's showdowns with the Red Baron aside, there are few traces of the war in American popular culture today, and no monument to the fallen adorns the National Mall in Washington, DC. The February 2011 death of America's last doughboy, the ambulance driver Frank Buckles, passed with only a smattering of commentary.

In Great Britain, by contrast, the war is truly the *Great* War. The poppies immortalized in John McCrae's 1915 poem "In Flanders Fields" remain a potent symbol of the dead, and red poppies, purchased to support the Royal British Legion, are still worn in lapels on Remembrance Sunday or laid in wreaths on war memorials big and small. So embedded is a basic understanding of the war in British culture that it has continued to serve over the past generation as a ready backdrop to popular television shows — from the BBC sitcom *Blackadder Goes Forth* to *Downton Abbey* — and to best-selling historical fiction by writers like Sebastian Faulks, Ben Elton, Pat Barker, and Ken Follett. The war's resonance in the former Dominions is, if anything, even stronger, as the sacrifices of Canadian and Anzac forces in the British war effort helped foster a sense of nationhood and prepare the way for full independence. "Anzac Day," celebrated with dawn services every April 25 to mark the anniversary of the 1915 Gallipoli landings, in which the Australian and New Zealand Army Corps suffered heavy losses, remains a solemn event in the Antipodes. Portions of "In Flanders Fields" (written by the Canadian McCrae) appear on the Canadian ten dollar bill; an image of a poppy has appeared on the quarter.

In France, efforts to commemorate those who died in defense of the nation in World War I — or, as happened during the 80th anniversary of the armistice, attempts to rehabilitate the memory of those who mutinied in 1917 — can still stir lively debates, a sure sign of the war's enduring significance for French national identity. In Germany, as in France and Britain, memorials to the local dead dot the countryside. Yet while the meaning of the Great War was vigorously contested in Weimar Germany prior to 1933, it has since been eclipsed by the Holocaust and World War II as an object of political dispute. When the war does enter German public discourse, it is usually less the conflict itself that is of interest than its position in a trajectory leading to the Third Reich. It is telling that the death of the last French *poilu*, the Verdun veteran Lazare Ponticelli, was honored by Nicolas Sarkozy with a state funeral in Les Invalides, while the passing of the last German veteran, Erich Kästner, escaped public notice for weeks and was ignored by German state authorities.

This diversity in the extent and forms of remembrance does not, however, correspond to much diversity in how the war is now commonly understood. Representations of the conflict today, and in the Anglophone world especially, tend to be versions of what has been called the "anti-war myth" of the Great War. The literary critic Samuel Hynes, who traced its construction in the tide of war novels and trench memoirs that began to appear a decade after the war's end, described this myth as "not a falsification of reality, but an imaginative version of it, the story of the war that has evolved, and has come to be accepted as true." Neither an objective portrayal nor a comprehensive account, the myth is "an idea of what the war was and what it meant."

The anti-war myth has grown so familiar — and, because it conforms to our collective expectations, so marketable — that it now stands virtually unchallenged as the common-sense view of the conflict. Ask someone what they think of when they think of World War I, and you will almost certainly encounter a predictable pastiche of gas attacks, muddy trenches, ubiquitous corpses, barbed wire, and terrifying high-explosive barrages. One envisions frightened young men, less agents in their own history than victims, sent "over the top" by incompetent generals, only to be mowed down by machine-gun fire. Those fortunate enough to survive this generational sacrifice returned home, one assumes, physically or psychologically scarred, and skeptical in either case of the values of the societies that had sent them to fight. Above all, it is the sheer suffocating senselessness of the war that rankles and sticks in the mind. As Captain Blackadder remarks in the aforementioned BBC series, just before being sent to his death in another futile attack, one could not even "get out of the war by pretending to be mad," since, after all, "who would have noticed another madman around here?"

This condemnation is the stock-in-trade of some of the best writing to emerge from the Great War. Its ingredients can be found in the works of such well-known witnesses as Robert Graves, Siegfried Sassoon, Wilfred Owen, and Henri Barbusse. Perhaps more than anything, it was Remarque's bestselling *All Quiet on the Western Front* (1929) which popularized the anti-war interpretation. The book told the story of earnest schoolboys lured into joining the war by the slick jingoism of their elders, only to have first their souls and then their lives snuffed out by forces of mechanized annihilation they can't begin to fathom. Remarque famously described the novel as an attempt "to tell of a generation of men who, even though they may have escaped shells, were destroyed by the war." But, as the historian Modris Eksteins has convincingly argued, the work is better read as evidence of its author's own postwar malaise, which he discovered how to pin on the war. Remarque, Eksteins claimed, "was more interested in explaining away the emotional imbalance of a generation than in a comprehensive or even accurate account of the experience and feelings of men in the trenches." Indeed, Remarque's wartime experience — he spent at most a month or two in the front lines — was far more limited than his novel led readers to suppose.

So influential were these depictions of doomed youth in a tragic war that Paul Fussell, in his classic *The Great War and Modern Memory*, could present their anxious and ironic tones, their sense of absurdity and powerlessness, as the 20th century's paradigmatic mode of truth-telling about war. "Every war is ironic," Fussell proclaimed,

> because every war is worse than expected... But the Great War was more ironic than any before or since. It was a hideous embarrassment to the prevailing Meliorist myth which had dominated the public consciousness for a century. It reversed the Idea of Progress.

Fussell's book, first published in 1975 in the shadow of Vietnam, is a good example of how, for readers already susceptible to this view of war, the very grimness of an account becomes an axiomatic guarantee of its truthfulness. In fact, at least part of the success of *The Great War in Modern Memory* — it won a National Book Award and, unusually for a work of literary criticism, was reprinted in a 25th anniversary edition in 2000 — seems traceable to its uncritical embrace of the anti-war myth.

It is important to recognize, however, that the anti-war myth has not always enjoyed such hegemony. In the 1920s and 1930s, it vied with a powerful "pro-war" position for interpretive rights to the conflict. For German writers (and veterans) like Ernst Jünger, Franz Schauwecker, Werner Beumelberg, and Edwin Dwinger, the war's violence was less victimizing than empowering. Life in the trenches had meant an experience of comradeship and newly awakened feelings of national belonging, and

an encounter with emotional intensities denied by the security of civilian life. Far from senseless suffering, the war had been a transcendent event, a revelation of the beauty of collective struggle and the nobility of self-sacrifice for high ideals. The war, Jünger declared in 1922, had created a "wholly new race, intelligent, strong, and full of will." Not all prophets of the pro-war myth were Germans, but it was in Germany that the pro-war myth bore its most sinister fruit, helping prepare the way for Hitler's rise to power.

Yet if the pro-war interpretation has aged poorly, discredited by its fascist associations, the anti-war position has only benefited from the passage of time. Subsequent wars have done little to dispel the popular belief that war is madness. The Cold War arms race, with its threat of an even more thorough and senseless apocalypse, along with the peace movements of the 1960s and 1970s, provided fertile soil for countless paperback editions of Remarque and popularizing statements of the anti-war case such as the epic 1964 BBC documentary *The Great War*. (With episodes entitled "For Such a Stupid Reason Too" and "Hell Cannot Be So Terrible," the series left little room for ambivalence.) The 1996 PBS/BBC co-production *The Great War and the Shaping of the 20th Century* reprised the argument in shorter form for a new generation. Among the clearest indications of the triumph of the anti-war narrative was the meeting, in 1984, of Helmut Kohl and François Mitterrand at a ceremony commemorating the dead at Verdun, long a symbol for the deranged logic of the entire conflict. More than a gesture of Franco-German reconciliation, their protracted handshake was a sign that the Great War's frightful lessons had finally been learned.

IT IS A CURIOUS FACT ABOUT THE GREAT WAR that one of its most important legacies was a highly politicized notion of the "war experience." The idea that the war had disclosed to its combatants a truth, one whose communication to the non-initiated was both urgent and difficult, was at the heart of each of the rival "myths" to which it gave birth. Whether the war experience was invoked to mobilize martial energies or to warn of future tragedies, whether it was celebrated as a quasi-sacred event or exposed as a horrifying agony, it was the authority of *those who were there* which captured the imagination and legitimized the message. The significance of the war and its essential experiences confirmed one another. More than any other conflict in modern times, the meanings ascribed to the Great War have hinged on the witness of common soldiers, on the testimony of what it was like to fight in places like Loos, Passchendaele, and Verdun.

Living memory, from which we expect not only the vividness of an experience but a moral too, has thus weighed more on our brains in the case of the Great War than we might suspect. To say that the memory of soldiers has mythologized the war is not to dismiss all claims; rather, it is to recognize that memory and experience are complexly related, and that recollection is colored by more than the events it relays. As the psychologist Daniel Schacter puts it, we do not so much "retrieve copies" of our experiences as "recreate or reconstruct" them. In doing so, we "bias our memories of the past by attributing to them emotions or knowledge we acquired after the event." The past self who experienced and the present self who remembers are not identical. The act of remembering even traumatic experiences can also be powerfully therapeutic, offering the chance to retrospectively transform the chaos and inscrutability of unfolding events into something like narrative coherence, from which their significance can then be read.

Like Remarque's *All Quiet on the Western Front*, many of the most famous accounts of fighting in World War I are postwar recollections in this sense: they interpret wartime experiences from a standpoint aware of how it all turned out, slotting incidents into a narrative arc only available after the fact. The gulf between immediate reactions and postwar attitudes could be extreme. As Samuel Hynes has pointed out, Robert Graves's description at the time of the day the war ended noted that "things were very quiet," with a "perfunctory" church service and "grouses about demobilization." A decade later, in his acclaimed memoir *Good-Bye to All That* (1929), Graves transformed the event into a highly literary scene of walking at night across ancient battlefields "cursing and sobbing and thinking of the dead."

One of the most revealing before-and-after comparisons has only recently become available. In 2010, Ernst Jünger's *Kriegstagebuch, 1914-1918* appeared in print, some 12 years after its author's death at the age of 102. This "War Diary," which records in meticulous detail Jünger's 44 months on the Western Front, formed the basis for a host of memoirs, of which *Storm of Steel* is undoubtedly the most famous. First published in 1920, *Storm of Steel* underwent numerous revisions, evolving throughout that decade into a manifesto of a "new nationalism" that recast Germany's battlefield defeat as a spiritual victory, the fiery birth of a new and hardened warrior-elite who would redeem the nation. Even in the amended 1961 edition on which the recent English translation is based, *Storm of Steel* remains an arresting counterpoint to the received wisdom about the war.

What is striking, however, is how this classic statement of the pro-war myth differs from the war Jünger recorded in his diaries. Indeed, the *Kriegstagebuch* reveals a soldier who, though clearly the narrator in embryo of works like *Storm of Steel*, was more susceptible to the war's grim absurdities than hitherto suspected. If the *Kriegstagebuch* never gives up on the war as a heroic adventure, it also records moments of clear disillusionment. As Jünger wrote in May 1917, in a meditation on the war's devastated landscape: "When will this shitty war come to an end? What might one have seen and enjoyed during this time… But still no end in sight."

There is, in fact, hardly a trope, image, or barb familiar to students of the anti-war myth that fails to find its way into the *Kriegstagebuch*. Jünger resents the orders of staff officers and begrudges ideas about the conduct of the war from those "rear-area pigs" less acquainted than he with conditions in the front lines. The gulf between the truth of actions Jünger has taken part in and the sanitized accounts that appear in official communiqués calls forth responses ranging from bemusement to disgruntled annoyance. Time and again he catalogs the miseries of rain, mud, cold, lice, boredom, shabby quarters, meager rations, interrupted sleep, and sheer exhaustion. And above all there is the ubiquitous presence of corpses: the soft feel of bodies beneath one's feet; the unmistakable smell of decomposing flesh, particularly unwelcome at mealtime; the sight and sound of maggots; bodies bloated and covered in flies; the discovery of corpses — or, more often, a mélange of their component parts — while digging in; and the relentless effects of artillery, disturbing and dismembering bodies long dead like a plow turning and breaking the soil. ("Not even the dead," Jünger dryly notes, "are permitted to rest in peace.") Death, when it comes, strikes randomly and from points unknown. That the liberal consumption of alcohol figures so prominently in Jünger's diaries is hardly a surprise.

Yet Jünger's *Kriegstagebuch* is by no means an "anti-war" document. His years of grief and squalor had been too leavened with redeeming moments — the "sporting" thrill of patrol, the pleasures of a "rough life among men," what Jünger calls the "magnificent spectacle" of devastated villages — to result in a rejection of the war. Its attitude can only be described as ambivalence. But if Jünger's later memories of the war privileged certain moments over others, it is because they sought to convey not just the documentary truth of the war, but its literary truth as well. They sought, in other words, a sense and coherence in the war experience which were only accessible once the war had been lost and the measure of the postwar world had been taken.

And herein lies an important lesson. It is not just that memories are made of flexible stuff. Nor is it that "experience," as the historian Joan Scott has argued, is less an objective source of knowledge than something whose invocation allows identities to take shape. (In Jünger's case, the political identity of a foe of Weimar democracy, whose position and message were grounded in a particular rendition of his "experience.") Rather, it is that sometimes living memory has to relax its grip on an event for the rest of us to discover it anew. Jünger's own living memory of the war — his desire, that is, to retain narrative control over the meaning of his experience — led him to brush off repeated requests to examine his original diary. Only in 1995, a few years before his death, was the diary made available to scholars. And only in 2009 was permission to publish received from his widow. Far from impoverishing our access to the reality of the trenches, Jünger's passing made available a source whose length, richness of description, and proximity to conditions of life at the front make it virtually unparalleled in the literature of the First World War.

THE FINAL DISAPPEARANCE of those who might tell us "I was there, and this is how it was" augurs a similar relaxation on a larger scale. With the centennial of the war's eruption just over the horizon and a flood of World War I books, cover stories, and documentaries about to break, there is hope that something more than genuflections to the old anti-war myth awaits us. For there is no question that our cultural memory of the war is but a selective fixation — in monuments, rites, symbols, and especially stories — of the more diverse memories once held by veterans themselves. Some tales become canonized while others are forgotten, and even famous accounts get read in one-dimensional ways. One forgets that Robert Graves disavowed "anti-war" intentions in writing *Good-Bye to All That*. Or that Henri Barbusse was opposed more to war in the abstract than to taking up arms in so just a cause as the crusade against German militarism. Or that Siegfried Sassoon, though tireless in his rebuke of the armchair warriors back home, was also a zealous officer famed for his bravery in confronting the enemy. One forgets, too, that some of the war's victims were also killers.

Scholars have been unraveling the anti-war myth for decades, but if the popular image of the Great War has failed to budge, this is partly because living memory has stood ready to confirm expectations. The oral historian Max Arthur's 2005 *Last Post*, which promised "the final word from our First World War soldiers," is a telling case, offering what is in fact a breviary of the anti-war myth. Thus the assertion of William Roberts (d. 2006) that "the Great War was a lot of political bull. There shouldn't be wars." Cecil Withers (d. 2005) echoed the sentiment, adding that "[t]hese days, if any trigger-happy politician wants to start another war, it's my job to let people know what that means." For Alfred Finnigan (d. 2005), World War I "started out idiotic and it stayed idiotic. It was damned silly, all of it." And Harry Patch, whose 2009 death occasioned anti-war poems and even an anti-war song by the English rock band Radiohead, lamented "[a]ll those lives lost for a war finished over a table. Now what is the sense in that?" Admonitions about the senselessness of war were in fact the universal tidings of the war's last veterans. As *Le Monde* reported in the wake of Lazare Ponticelli's death in 2008, his final years were devoted to delivering the message: "To the children, I say and I repeat: do not make war."

These are, and will remain, testimonies worthy of reflection. It would be perverse to deny that war is a source of tragedy, and dangerous to glorify it. But the trouble is that such warnings slide too easily into the grooves of a long-established narrative, and the witness they bear creates obstacles to uncluttered thinking, not only about the Great War, but about war in general. Instead, we are left with spectacles like Steven Spielberg's saccharine 2011 film *War Horse*, noteworthy only for its novel extension of the anti-war myth to the animal kingdom. Even as tremendous a book as Dexter Filkins' *The Forever War* (2008), based on his time as a war correspondent in Iraq, cannot resist ending its account of America's war against Islamic fundamentalism with a visit to a World War I-era British cemetery in Baghdad. Walking among the graves of soldiers fallen in the Mesopotamian campaign against the Ottomans, Filkins quietly permits the scene to suggest a similar dearth of sense and purpose in America's misadventures in the same land some 90 years later. Again, the Great War is reflexively trotted out as a metaphor for war's vain wastage of human lives.

The reality of the World War I "experience," like the reality of the experience of any war, was more complex. Charles Carrington, whose *A Subaltern's War* (1929), published under the pseudonym "Charles Edmonds," deserves to be better known, provides a corrective. Indeed, Carrington, a veteran of the bloody Somme and Passchendaele offensives, makes plain that the baffling question why men continued to fight such a war of attrition only really perplexes from the vantage point of the anti-war myth. In an epilogue to the first edition that took aim at the "literary fashion in war books," Carrington declared that "it is not honest to deny the existence of happiness which was actually derived from the war." Horrors and hardships were hardly continuous, he pointed out, and they were balanced by the pleasures of rest, the chance for adventure, and the comforts of comradeship.

For Carrington, the "moment of disenchantment" only arrived after the peace was signed. It was then that "the spell which had bound us for such a long time was broken; the charm failed; an illusion came crashing down about our ears and left us in an unfamiliar world." *A Subaltern's War* was Carrington's attempt to tell a more candid story. "No corrupt sergeant majors," he wrote, "stole my rations or accepted my bribes. No incompetent colonels failed to give me food or lodging. No casual staff officers ordered me to certain death, indifferent to my fate."

It would, however, be no less wrong to present the honest ambivalence of Carrington, or Ernst Jünger, as emblematic of the "war experience." The underwhelming truth is that there is no such thing as a single representative story of the Great War. Anyone interested in the diversity of testimonies that emerged from the war (and the pressures and motives that shaped them) need only consult Leonard Smith's *The Embattled Self: French Soldiers' Testimonies of the Great War* (2007) or Brian Bond's *Survivors of a Kind: Memoirs of the Western Front* (2008). "The truism of tragedy and victimization in the Great War," Smith argues, "certainly enables us to interpret testimony clearly, but at the cost of closing off our understanding of the creativity with which soldiers grappled with their predicament." Part of this "creativity" involved recourse to a host of narrative strategies to make sense of their wartime experience — as a rite of passage, say, or a tale of "mastering" the extremes of death and disfigurement — all essentially different from the more familiar moralizing narratives of tragedy and trauma. Bond likewise demonstrates "the tremendous variety of war memoirs in, for example, their style of presentation and in their authors' attitudes to the war, beyond the handful of classics admitted to the literary canon." These include "unapologetic warriors" like Alfred Pollard, author of *Fire-Eater* (1932), who relished the war as a chance for martial glory; and Frederic Manning's masterful *Her Privates We* (1930), which unsentimentally depicts the scrounging, scrimshanking, gossiping, and boozing of common soldiers, whose exhaustion and grim resolve to do their duty give the lie to any simple notions about "disenchantment."

The reader of these works might also reflect on whether the cause of peace today is best served by recycling myths about war. For one thing seems clear: cloaking the Great War in a mystique of incomprehensible horror has not made war any less likely, or any more humane. Like all such auras, the anti-war myth may even exercise a dark fascination. As François Truffaut is supposed to have said, there is no such thing as an anti-war film, since the action of warfare, however barbarous, cannot fail to excite. What is decidedly not served, in any case, is the task of understanding, which involves the uncomfortable recognition that war can mean a good deal more than just senseless agony. A sober anti-war position ought to concern itself not only with war's horrors but with its attractions: what leads people to go off to fight in the first place, and — crucially — to continue once they're there.

It matters, after all, whether World War I soldiers remained in the trenches through "coercion" or "consent" (to borrow terms from an ongoing revisionist debate). It matters, in other words, to how one plans to prevent the next war whether one believes that millions were led to the slaughter by self-serving politicians and heartless generals, or whether one thinks millions died as self-conscious defenders of nations and empires in causes they believed were just. As Leonard Smith has put it, to pay attention to forms of consent is to stress "the internalization on the part of millions of Europeans in and out of uniform of at least some of the values for which they claimed the war had to be fought." Employing the notion of "war cultures," historians of the consent school ask about the beliefs and symbols which made the Great War seem worth fighting, and which led contemporaries to stick it out even as the conflict's unforeseen brutality became clear. If support for the Great War was at times manufactured and cajoled, it was also often negotiated, argued for, acquiesced in, and granted in full awareness of the risks involved. For soldiers in the 1914-18 war, consent could mean the duty of citizenship, obligations to tribe or family, defending the homeland, loyalty to comrades, or even the chance for excitement and escape from civilian life — none of which adds up to the cliché of a pointless war or a tale of passive victimization. Combatants were driven not only by "sticks," as historian Niall Ferguson has noted, but by "carrots" too.

Far from a surrender to militarism, gaining critical distance on the anti-war myth of the Great War can help bring perspective to today's anti-war politics. With public opinion now against the Iraq War — a recent Gallup poll found that 53 percent of Americans consider the March 2003 invasion a mistake, compared to only 24 percent at the time — another powerful narrative of tragedy and trauma is beginning to ossify. The skeleton of this new anti-war myth was already present in Michael Moore's 2003 Oscar acceptance speech (delivered as bombs were falling on Baghdad), which damned George W. Bush as a "fictitious president" who took us "to war for fictitious reasons." Moore's 2004 film *Fahrenheit 9/11* married this indictment to charges of incompetence, monied influence, and indifference to the unjustified suffering inflicted on soldiers and families. A raft of disillusioned Iraq War memoirs — Paul Rieckhoff's *Chasing Ghosts*, Brandon Friedman's *The War I Always Wanted*, and Michael Anthony's *Mass Casualties*, among others — have since appeared which can provide this view with the authenticating voice of direct experience. The U.S. occupation now over, the swirl of stories and claims can settle into a common-sense idea of the war as yet another futile debacle wrought by generals and politicians.

But like the anti-war myth of the Great War, this interpretation isn't so much wrong as simplistic, and even comforting, in its unambiguous assignment of blame. For a response to the Iraq War that is not mythopoeic, but rather demythologizing, we might look to a different, if no less outraged, anti-war speech. This was the commencement address delivered by journalist Chris Hedges at Rockford College in May 2003. Hedges, a former war correspondent, spoke of the allure and moral corrosion of war, themes elaborated in his 2002 book *War Is a Force That Gives Us Meaning*. Without letting the Bush administration off the hook, Hedges observed Americans' collective self-exaltation as we watched "Shock and Awe" and delighted in televised proof of our military power. In an admonition that applies equally to soldiers and civilians, he argued that the "seduction of war is insidious because so much of what we are told about it is true — it does create a feeling of comradeship which obliterates our alienation and makes us, for perhaps the only time in our life, feel we belong." Faced with scandals and deficits and the tragedy of 9/11, Americans found in war a diversion, a feeling of nobility and selflessness, and "that ecstatic bliss that comes with belonging to a crowd in wartime." Hedges' audience, as though obliged to corroborate this censure, answered with a barrage of hisses and defiant chants of "USA! USA!"

Whether or not future generations will remember the Iraq War as another "pointless" war is uncertain. Yet Hedges, by reminding us of at least some of the deep sources of our support for war, prompts us to ask the questions that can forestall any facile mythmaking. How, as soldiers or civilians, did we consent to the invasion and long occupation of Iraq? More importantly: how, as a nation, do we continue to allow our identities and meanings to be invested in war? It may be that we can best mark the centennial of the Great War and honor the suffering it caused by resisting the urge to mythologize our own wars, whether as paradises or infernos. After all, such myths have proven a poor prophylaxis against renewed outbreaks of war fever.

"Can war be prevented?" Charles Carrington asked in 1929. He answered in the affirmative, but added the following disclaimer:

> We shall cease to fight to the death so soon as we rid our hearts of envy, hatred, and malice. Since this seems improbable at the moment... we can take precautions just as we take them against shipwreck. Among these will not be found vote-catching treaties, abuse of friendly nations, jeers and sneers against the police work done by soldiers and sailors, misrepresentation of the facts about war, nor any of the seven-devils which may enter when the devil of militarism is driven out. ✦

DEATH

RIGOBERTO GONZÁLEZ

Our grandparents lived down the street from the town's only cemetery, and when we passed by at night my brother and I liked to dare one another to walk close to the gate. Every Sunday, always the childish prodding and pushing. When our grandparents died, they were buried in that cemetery, and so our visits changed tune, slightly. We made a game of hiding behind the tombstones and swatting each other with brittle roses, making petal explosions with our heads. We grew older. And many years later we buried my brother, a military soldier, in that cemetery, after his body was delivered. My aging parents moved into that house just up the road, and I, a childless bachelor, made the trips alone. Once I heard my brother and me laughing inside the cemetery, and when I turned my head so quickly that I strained a muscle in my neck, I felt foolish. It was simply two other children doing what we had done those many years ago. Was it a bead of sweat or a tear that jumped on my nose when I snapped to attention? The insect that landed on it and soaked it up knows the answer, but it too went away and vanished among the graves and wreaths and decay.

Flatland: On Javier Marías

BEN MAUK

I COME IN PRAISE OF FLATNESS, and to suggest that "flat" is the word for the novels of Javier Marías, though it's one deployed by critics almost always to diminish, rather than to praise. E.M. Forster famously warns against peopling a story with too many "flat" (i.e. Dickensian) characters, and after him stands an army of Goodreads bloggers ready to use the word to describe prose that, like a Coke abandoned in the rain, lacks sufficient fizz. At best, one finds John Gardner suggesting in *The Art of Fiction* that stylistic flatness "may be a virtue" in the limited case of "*New Yorker* 'super-realist' fiction" (whatever that is).

Not all flatnesses are created equal, of course, nor are they defined equally well. Forgetting for a moment the special case of flat characters — a concept Forster valiantly attempts to clarify against its rounded counterpart — it is often unclear whether the critic has defined for himself the flaw he's busy decrying. What does Henry James find flat in Flaubert's "A Simple Heart"? Is it akin to what Philip Pullman criticizes in Dan Brown's "flat, stunted and ugly prose"? A provisional list of these flatnesses might include language choices that simply fail to strike the ear or eye, sensory descriptions that encourage skimming, charmless dialogue, rote exposition, dryness, even a lack of emotional vibrancy. Though no doubt incomplete, all of these flatnesses seem to be manifestations of the same essential phenomenon: a failure of the writer's words to leap aggressively from the page and into the reader's memory — a failure, in other words, to distinguish one line (or sentence, or scene…) from the next.

Those flatnesses may be distant cousins to Marías's rarified strain, but their similarities have nevertheless dissuaded critics from praising his writing by invoking the quality that most obviously defines it. He is called "maximalist" and "digressive," "philosophical" and "flowery," but never flat. Yet more than any living writer, his work exemplifies that so-called failure.

Marías's novels began appearing in English over two decades ago. It may be only now, with the much-hyped publication of *The Infatuations*, his 13th, that he achieves the sort of mainstream success in the United States that he has long enjoyed in Spain. If he does, it will be thanks to his uncelebrated flatness, through which he manages to create worlds as rich, subtle, and hypnotic as our own.

Consider a typical paragraph from *The Infatuations*. This opening of an early chapter finds the narrator, an editorial assistant named María Dolz, at the apartment of a bereaved widow whom she barely knows but has often observed from afar, and who moments ago was lamenting the loss of her husband:

> She fell silent and looked over at the adjoining room where the children were. The television was on in the background, so it seemed that everything was fine. From what I'd seen of them, they were well-brought-up kids, far more so than children usually are nowadays. Curiously, I didn't find it surprising or embarrassing that Luisa should speak to me so openly, as if I were a friend. Perhaps she couldn't talk about anything else, and in the intervening months since Deverne's death, she had exhausted all those closest to her with her shock and anxieties, or she felt awkward about going on and on at them, always harping on about the same thing, and was taking advantage of the novelty of my presence there to vent her feelings. Perhaps it didn't matter who I was, it was enough that I was there, an as yet unused interlocutor, with whom she could start afresh. That's another of the problems when one suffers a misfortune: the effects on the victim far outlast the patience of those prepared to listen and accompany her, unconditional support never lasts very long once it has become tinged with monotony. And so, sooner or later, the grieving person is left alone when she has still not finished grieving or when she's no longer allowed to talk about what remains her only world, because other people find that grief unbearable, repellant. She understands that for them sadness has a social expiry date, that no one is capable of contemplating another's sorrow, that such a spectacle is tolerable only for a brief period, for as long as the shock and pain last and there is still some role for those who are watching, who then feel necessary, salvatory, useful. But on discovering that nothing changes and that the affected person neither progresses nor emerges from her grief, they feel humiliated and superfluous, they find it almost offensive and stand aside: "Aren't I enough for you? Why can't you climb out of that pit with me by your side? Why are you still grieving when time has passed and I've

> been here all the while to console and distract you? If you can't climb out, then sink or disappear." And the grieving person does just that, she retreats, removes herself, hides. Perhaps Luisa clung to me that afternoon because with me she could be what she still was, with no need for subterfuge: the inconsolable widow, to use the usual phrase. Obsessed, boring, grief-stricken.

The paragraph is standard length for Marías — if anything, it's on the short side — and showcases many of the flattening features that crop up on almost every page of his work: scant sensory detail, essayistic rhetoric, an analytical and emotionless voice, and smooth transitions from scene into deadpan psychological analysis, and back again. Marías rarely uses a paragraph break to signal a move into the narrator's mind. (Another writer might do so just before "Curiously, I...") Such rhythms are instead accomplished by his unorthodox use of the comma splice, which marks moments of toggling between scenic and ruminative modes, and between divergent variations on an observed or imagined event. We follow the narrator, comma by comma, as she circles around and revises her position, often by adding clauses ("they feel humiliated and superfluous, they find it almost offensive") or by multiplying a description with clarifying alternatives to a chosen word ("other people find that grief unbearable, repellant"; "necessary, salvatory, useful"; "Obsessed, boring, grief-stricken"). Yet because the splice may be performing one of several functions, we can never predict whether a sentence is about to veer back into scene, or continue to accumulate modal possibilities.

The paragraph is also typical for its inclusion of an imagined mini-scene, complete with invented dialogue (" 'Aren't I enough for you?' "), so that the reader is forced to accompany Dolz's train of thought as she seems to "zone out" in the middle of Luisa's living room to some undisclosed, half-realized daydream sequence. Skimming here would be unadvisable, lest you confuse what takes place in the narrator's mental sandbox with what is taking place in the book's "reality" — after all, the two may differ only nominally, and may be separated by little more than a lone comma. This stylistic blurring is quite intentional, not to mention psychologically acute. Who hasn't, during the private postmortem of a cocktail party or sexual encounter, imputed to a person what we merely feared or hoped they might say? In such scenarios Marías's characters, and moreover his readers, are in constant danger of eyewitness unreliability. They enact the mind's tendency to confuse the real and counterfactual.

For Marías, scenes behave like fantasies, thoughts like dialogue, reflection like action. The usual effects that writers employ against flatness, and which also serve to demarcate the internal and external worlds of a novel, are absent here. Like a novelty rest-stop penny, the various narrative modes are flattened under the pressure of the protagonist's attention, until each resembles the other. The resulting distortion is a depiction of the improvisatory life of the mind and its blurred relationship to the world: a remarkable effect accomplished by his sanding down to nothing the stylistic and dramatic markers that, in conventional narration, make clear the distance between world and dream.

The Infatuations IS MARÍAS'S FIRST NOVEL to be narrated by a woman (an experiment that, in his 2006 interview with *The Paris Review*, he claimed he would never try) but otherwise follows in the mold of many of his previous books, placing an inscrutable, educated loner into a pulpy and violent premise. On the first page of his breakout novel *A Heart So White* (1992), a young newlywed excuses herself from lunch, enters a bathroom, and shoots herself in the chest. *Tomorrow in the Battle Think on Me* (1994) opens as a would-be adulterous wife dies unexpectedly in her would-be lover's arms, forcing him to improvise a quick escape. The novella *Bad Nature, or With Elvis in Mexico* (1996) commences with the raving monologue of a hunted man, and in the three-volume epic *Your Face Tomorrow* (2002–2007), a taciturn spy is drawn into progressively bloodier escapades, each of which receives the usual exhaustive commentary.

The Infatuations inhabits this same universe of analysis and intrigue, and even revisits some of the names and recurring characters Marías's readers have come to expect. New to the world is genial voyeur María Dolz, the editorial assistant, who every morning before work watches a married couple, Miguel and Luisa Desvern, eating in a Madrid café. Most of Marías's protagonists are unabashed people-watchers, and Dolz hardly needs to defend her hobby, although of course she does, and at length: "It comforted me to breathe the same air and to be a part — albeit unnoticed — of their morning landscape, before they went their separate ways."

The plot is absurdly simple and can be dispensed with in a few lines. First, Dolz learns that Miguel has been brutally murdered by a raving lunatic, in what the newspapers describe as a random assault. Soon enough, she works up the courage to approach Luisa, and their brief conversation leads to an invitation to the couple's apartment, where Dolz meets and falls for the family friend who has taken it upon himself to care for the bereaved family.

Of course, because this is Marías, we know right away that Miguel's murder cannot be a random occurrence; his novels involve so few events that each must be positioned to withstand several successive theories and counter-theories, the internal composition of which forms the bulk of the text. It's no surprise, then, that Dolz's tenuous romance leads her to discover facts that complicate and disturb her picture of the Desverns' relationship, and especially the circumstances surrounding the husband's death. The surprises in Marías are never what or how, but why.

PSYCHOLOGICAL ACUITY ASIDE, the peculiar flatness of Marías's prose also functions to distinguish his universe from those of the supermarket thrillers his plots superficially resemble. (Those books may be flat in the fizzless sense, I suppose.) His attentions feel wrought from another era, and *The Infatuations* in particular reads as though Henry James had been commissioned to write the novelization of a lost Hitchcock film. As so often in Hitchcock (*Rear Window*, *Vertigo*, *North by Northwest*, and *The Man Who Knew Too Much* all come quickly to mind), Dolz becomes embroiled, through a combination of curiosity and kindness, in a sinister plot over which she has no control. She is driven into the Desverns' lives because she is entranced by their apparent bliss, yet it is her feelings of pity for Luisa that cause her to approach the widow, and that later motivate her investigation into Miguel's murder. And as with Hitchcock's heroes, Dolz endangers herself with little more than good intentions and a too-keen eye and ear.

The James connection is stylistically overt in that, throughout the novel, the suspense of wondering whether Dolz will escape a scenario unharmed is regularly superseded by the suspense of wondering when and how a particularly labyrinthine sentence will end. But Marías also shares James's interest in exploring the many faces of a single personality flaw, variously manifested in each of the main characters: in *The Infatuations*, that flaw is envy, the definition of which Luisa at one point reads to Dolz out of an old dictionary. And though it may be incidental, Marías also resembles his predecessor in his willingness to embrace "un-literary" genres: for James, horror; for Marías, suspense.

But *The Infatuations* is more concerned with its thoughts on jealousy, mortality, and intimacy than with the thrills of physical danger, even if Dolz's snooping leads her into a handful of precarious, and parodic, set pieces. (At one point, she contrives to walk half-naked into a room where two murderers are talking, so as to indicate to them that she was not eavesdropping on their damning conversation, or even aware of their presence.) In these situations Marías's flattening style serves a third purpose: building suspense, which by itself is no mean feat. It may be significant that few remember the novel and short story on which *Vertigo* and *Rear Window* are respectively based. Prolonging tension in a scene without trying the reader's patience or resorting to tired gimmicks is as difficult to achieve in fiction as it is in film. Here, Marías has mastered it with Hitchcockian confidence.

So IT SEEMS THAT, WHEN PRESSED, one can invent dramatic as well as psychological justifications for Marías's flatness. Yet the overall effect remains uncanny. *The Infatuations* shouldn't succeed: for a thriller, there are few surprises or plot twists, and the failed romance of the book's second half is cheaply contrived to reveal the circumstances of Desvern's death; for a work of literature, the plot is pulpy, the motives soap operatic. What's more, most of the characters are broad types whose innermost thoughts we feel we know immediately, or else, in the case of the narrator, inscrutable objects who remain obscure to the very end. And worst of all, these faults are typical of the Marías-verse: *none* of his books should succeed! They ought to plod along, excruciatingly slow and measured, thoroughly unbelievable, as flat and dull as packed dirt.

James Wood has praised the novel form as "the great virtuoso of exceptionalism"; it always wriggles out of the constraints critics invent in their quest to define and limit the Good. More so than any living writer, Marías has wriggled out of the novelist's received truths about flatness, monotony, and repetition. It may be that when critics warn against flatness they are in fact decrying something else entirely, which often — but not always — accompanies flatness, and that renders our experience of the writing as reductive or dull. In fact, the thing may simply *be* dullness. Presumably this connotation is why Clancy Martin, in his recent review of Tao Lin's *Taipei* for *The New York Times*, describes that book's prose as "simple but never flat." Clearly, he means to say "simple but never *dull*."

Marías's flatness has nothing to do with simplicity. In fact, the flatness of his fiction — specifically, the way his narrative modes lie flush up against one another — is what allows hidden complexities to emerge from the slightest of plots. Marías has turned the "flaw" of flatness into a device that allows his characters to envision the world as an expanse of possibilities, counterfactuals, and anticipations. The result is a remarkably multivalent reading experience. On finishing *The Infatuations*, one feels part of an intricate, gemlike formation, composed of surfaces both the writer's and one's own by some improbable act of literary crystallography: each flatness reflecting another, culminating in sharpness, brilliance, depth. ✦

Clueless about what to do on your commute? Listen to thousands of mysteries.
Try Audible with a free audiobook at audible.com/larb
audible
an amazon company
Available on the App Store
Google play
Membership billed monthly, cancel anytime.

Coast Highway
ORCORAN
South on Pacific Coast Highway
GARY PAUL CORCORAN
A jaded private detective.
The Southern California coastline.
Four dead bodies and a search for Zen amidst the detritus of modern existence.
Now Available for
$3.99 on
KINDLE NOOK IBOOKS
and all other e-publications sites.
Award winning novelist and poet, Carolyn Howard-Johnson, says, "Women will love the heart and soul of one Michael Devlin …summertime's #1 beach read …pick up a tube of #60 SPF …South on Pacific Coast Highway is one crime story you won't be able to put down!"
Fran Lewis of JustReviews says of author Gary Paul Corcoran and his charmingly off the cuff PI, Michael Devlin, "A great author, a spell binding novel and one must read!"
Read reviews on goodreads
GARYPAULCORCORAN.COM

UGLY
DUCKLING
PRESSE
WHO ARE YOU READING?

A STORY OF ISLAM, PAKISTAN, FAMILY, AND WAR
BY SHAHAN MUFTI
"THIS IS A HISTORY OF PAKISTAN from the pen of a keen observer, whose own story represents Pakistan's past and whose vision reflects its hope for the future."
—VALI NASR, author of The Dispensable Nation
The Faithful Scribe
A STORY OF ISLAM, PAKISTAN, FAMILY AND WAR
SHAHAN MUFTI
OTHERPRESS.COM